RESEARCH FROM THE ALBAN INSTITUTE

HOW TO BUILD A SUPPORT SYSTEM FOR YOUR MINISTRY

ROY M. OSWALD

D1319579

The Publications Program of The Alban Institute is assisted by a grant from Trinity Church, New York City.

Library of Congress Catalog Card #90-86200.

CONTENTS

PREFACE

I look forward to the day when a parent will call her child to her side and say, "Hey, Son/Daughter, sit for a moment. I'm going to teach you how to go out into society and build a support network for yourself. This is probably the most important thing I'm going to teach you."

Because I don't think that day is coming soon, I have written this book as a step along the path to such a moment.

Knowing what I do now about the importance of support in our lives for health, sanity, and job effectiveness, I'm surprised that little or nothing about support is taught to us anywhere in our formal education. We can't live without it, yet it is as taken for granted as the air we breathe.

The need for support becomes especially obvious when, in our need, we look around us, only to discover that we are all alone. For me the need for support was most obvious in my early years as a parish pastor. What a difference an ongoing support group would have made to my ministry then. I believe this so strongly that I wish I could go back and start over again—only this time I would put some hard, intentional work into building a support network before diving into ministry and getting lost.

Since those early years, but especially in the last ten years, I have been much more intentional about the task of building support. I've also learned some things about what works and what doesn't. Along the way I've discovered Bruce Reed's Oscillation Theory, which has helped me to understand more clearly why some peer support groups work and others don't. I was fortunate in having a research project come my way in which I was able to test some of these theories of support. Carlisle Presbytery in central Pennsylvania came to The Alban Institute four years ago to ask us to help them deal with a clergy morale problem.

When we suggested experimenting with the development of more effective clergy peer groups, they decided to give it a try. Much of what follows centers around my learning in that research project.

I want to acknowledge my gratitude to Dorothy Yingling, who spearheaded the development of the Carlisle project. Her initial concern for the well-being of the clergy in that presbytery got the project under way. I have come to know her as a competent, retired corporate executive who wanted to turn her expertise to tackling some of the key problems facing the church today. I admire her love for the church and her deep conviction that church systems could be much more effective in supporting ministry. She has thrown herself into the fray and proved that she was right. I am grateful also for her appreciation of the work of The Alban Institute and her willingness to serve on our board of trustees.

I am writing this book especially for all those clergy who feel they are dangling by a rope on the side of a cliff without anyone around to help them climb back up. I know it would be nice if support came with the job, but it doesn't. If you want support for the work of your ministry, you will have to build your own support network. Even though no one told you that you needed to do this, it is foolhardy to begin ministry without this first step. This book will help you do just that. The cliff is worth scaling, but it's a whole lot easier and more fun when there are people around who believe in you and what you are trying to do. Here's to building a solid support network for yourself.

CHAPTER I

Clergy Support Systems

Looking back on my life as an ordained minister, I am acutely aware of the breadth, depth, and richness of the support system that now undergirds my life and work, and how sparse the support system was in my early years of ministry, which were accompanied by isolation, loneliness, and professional ineffectiveness. The overview allows me to see the direct correlation between the quality of support that surrounds the individual and personal and professional competence.

My current level of high support has not happened by accident. Through my work with The Alban Institute and the Clergy in Transition Research, I became aware of a key myth that I had lived with for years, namely that support systems happen by accident. It is a myth that I continually encounter when I work with clergy groups. The myth contains the naive assumption that all you need to do is work hard and maintain high integrity, and there will always be people around to support you. As a result of this insight, whenever it was appropriate, I began building into clergy seminars a time when the participants could critique the breadth and depth of their support systems and develop some intentionality about altering the quality of support in their lives. Because we all learn best by teaching what we need to learn, I have put some hard, intentional work into building and maintaining the high level of support I now feel in my life. More on how I did this later.

My Life Without Support

For the present I want to reflect on my early years as a parish pastor when I felt completely devoid of support. Actually, a lot more support was probably available to me at the time, but I either didn't know it or didn't know how to draw from that support what I needed.

I recall an incident in my first parish in Canada, where I had been working rather intensely with a particular woman of the parish who had many personal and family problems. She had run out on her husband and kids several times, but had been doing fairly well for two years. One afternoon at the conclusion of a counseling session in her living room, I got up to leave and she asked me to sit beside her for a while on the davenport. I complied, but when I got up to leave a second time, she reached up, cradled my head, and pulled me down toward her. Completely shocked, I struggled free, put on my coat, and left the house without saying a word. I recall the dismay and confusion I felt as I drove home. On the one hand, I was sexually aroused by the experience. On the other hand, I was completely undone by the realization that the two years of intense work I had been doing with her was flawed at a primary level. Apparently this parishioner loved the attention I gave her on a weekly basis, which would have discontinued once she "got well." My enmeshed, overly responsive pastoral style was actually contributing to her remaining dysfunctional because in that way she could continue to ensure my personal attention.

In reflecting on that incident I am aware that there was no one with whom I felt I could share my dismay, confusion, and pain. Reluctant to share my confusion about my own sexual arousal, I decided against sharing the incident with my wife. Being open with some of my fellow clergy in that city seemed out of the question. The one ecumenical clergy Bible study and sermon preparation group that met weekly was not into sharing personal pain and confusion. I felt I knew what they would say about that sort of thing, and I didn't need to appear too much of a naive novice in their eyes.

It was a little different with the close friendships with colleagues whom I met once or twice a year at a synod level. Under the right circumstances I might have brought it up, but there was rarely the time or the occasion. We desperately needed to get out of our roles and play a little. Besides that, I had no clear vision of how much I really needed some help in debriefing that experience and getting back on track in some kind of helpful role with my parishioner. As it was, I left that pastorate a year later and never really did talk through that incident with my parishioner. We remain alienated. I have recounted that incident several times in settings with other clergy when the subject came up about "parishioners being on the make" for their pastor. Yet even now, twenty-four years later, I would benefit from an hour-long case study session on that particular incident in ministry. I still carry some pain and disgust with myself about the missed opportunity for a much more effective pastoral response following that break in relationship.

That is just one of many critical incidents in ministry that I muddled through with anxiety and confusion. There was only one time that I can remember when I made a decision to see my Anglican colleague about a dilemma that was bewitching me. I asked for advice and he gave it, which was not really what I needed at the time. I really needed someone to help me think through my various options and what kinds of feelings I had about each. This is generally the kind of assistance offered through a support group. With all the remaining issues that confused and perplexed me, I proceeded on the assumption I had learned well in seminary, i.e., that I should be able to manage those issues on my own.

I recall the pain and confusion I experienced in the marital conflicts that resulted from the intensity I brought to my pastoral tasks. I believed I needed to be out visiting every evening of the week. On weekends I was a whirlwind of activity around the parish. My former wife and I simply had very little time together, and when we were together I was usually too exhausted to give much energy to the relationship. Because I was so unconnected with other clergy on any deep level, I automatically assumed that all clergy worked as hard as I did.

Late one evening about 2:00 a.m. I come downstairs because I could not sleep. I rarely cry, but through the tears in my eyes I spied my home communion kit sitting on the coffee table. I felt so empty and exhausted that I wondered if I might administer the Holy Communion to myself. I needed something to nurture me, and I felt as though God had simply abandoned me. I found myself dismissing the thought of offering myself the Eucharist because I had been taught that the Sacrament was to be used in the context of community; therefore, it was not something you gave to yourself. How different all this could have been for me if I had been part of a group of colleagues who met every two weeks to share pain, confusion, and joy.

When it came time to decide whether I should leave the parish in Canada and come to the United States to pursue a career in youth ministry (my goal in life at the time), I had to struggle through that decision all by myself as well. My Canadian colleagues gave little support to my plan of leaving for the fleshpots of the United States. There were no seasoned colleagues who might have suggested that I pay attention to the way I closed out in that parish, nor anyone to warn me about the emotional kick in the gut I would receive upon leaving my first parish. There were also no peers to share the anguish I went through in deciding whether to leave or not, or to help me deal with the guilt I felt at leaving a beloved congregation that had seen me through my first stumbling steps in ministry.

Once I left that parish for a new position south of the border, I did fare better in receiving support. One big advantage on reaching Pennsylvania was becoming part of a synod staff of fourteen professionals, each with a portfolio of responsibility. Mine was youth ministry. The key difference this time was that I had a mentor who served on the staff with me in the synod offices and who was approximately fifteen years older than I. Ira Sassaman was not always there when I felt I needed him, but he certainly was there for me at the times when I really did need him. Whenever I was confronted with a problem or had gotten myself into trouble, there was always Ira to drop in to see. Somehow the issues or problems never seemed so big when I left his office.

Mentors: Anchors in a Stormy Sea

Not enough is written about the importance of mentors in ministry, especially for those entering new roles and areas of responsibility. In the book *Beyond the Boundary*,[1] the three other authors and I work at some delineation of this most important role in the life of persons new to parish ministry. We try to distinguish between a mentor, a role model, and a pastoral colleague. When discussing support for professional competence in a complex role, I am very much aware of how important certain mentors were to me following those first five years in ministry when I didn't have any. The difference between not having and having mentors is similar to the difference between being sent on your own to find out where you fit into a new school system as a fourth-grader in a new city, and having your big brother take you to your new classroom. Either way you must make it on your own in the new class situation. Yet what a difference it makes when you have a big brother or sister who knows what you are going through and who personally sees to it that you get off to a good start.

Daniel Levinson in his book *The Seasons of a Man's Life* talks fairly extensively about younger men who are lucky enough to have mentors. In his research, which is now also being done with women, those who had mentors attained career goals much more easily than those who did not. Levinson makes it sound as though mentors are an important ingredient for professionals who need to acquire some essential skills quickly and early in their careers.

Nothing in our training for ministry assists us in integrating all we are learning into a particular style of ministry. Seminary throws information and ideas at us piecemeal. During my ministerial training, no one attempted to help me integrate the theology, Bible, and history I was learning with pastoral care and my own particular personality, with its strengths and weaknesses. While an intern I was to give this a provisional try, with persons giving me feedback. I don't want to minimize the value of that attempt. Clinical Pastoral Education was another setting in which who I was as a whole person was considered a key to how I functioned as a pastor. During each of these situations, as well as on my own following ordination, it was mentors of my choosing who were able to provide me a model of how I might put it all together into a style of doing ministry. It was not that I necessarily emulated and adopted their style wholesale. Rather, I was able to see how someone else integrated learnings and experiences into a style of ministry so that I could then figure out how I wanted to execute the role.

How different those opening years in the parish would have been if I had found myself such a mentor and contracted to spend one day a month with him. Just being able to follow him around as he visited parishioners in the hospital or called on shut-ins or dealt with a death in a family would have made all the difference in the world. In the absence of that person I had to "find my own way to school."

While in Pennsylvania I had two mentors who had a great influence on my development into the professional in ministry that I am now. The most helpful was my friend and colleague Ira Sassaman. The other mentor was a fellow Lutheran pastor who had acquired skill and reputation as a human relations specialist. Otto Kroeger was my guru as I began picking up knowledge and skill in the whole area of the applied behavioral sciences. He was a great trainer and group facilitator, and I always learned something simply by watching him interact with the people around him or confront interpersonal or group conflict. Aside from professional skills, Otto always appeared to be enjoying himself, whatever he was doing. Life with Otto is a laugh a minute. He taught me a lot about loosening up a little and enjoying life.

My eight years as director of youth ministry on the synod staff in Pennsylvania were stormy. During the 1960s it was difficult to be engaged with young people and not to be deep in controversy. Unfortunately, I was not one to do things halfway. If the war in Vietnam was engaging our youth in a morally questionable enterprise, then it ought to be stopped. Hence much of my time was spent in draft resistance counseling and demonstrating against the war on the streets of Harrisburg. I was quickly painted as the radical on the synod staff. I found myself actively despised by a large portion of the foremost clergy and lay leaders in the synod. The executive board of the synod made several attempts to have me censured. The bishop was given lots of encouragement to have me fired. Fortunately I had enough support within the system to block that. In the peace effort there was strong support from a small, ecumenical band that continued to press for the war's end.

When my marriage fell apart I knew I needed to leave. Fortunately for me, this time there was a cadre of supporters who carried me through the dark hole of feeling like a failure professionally as well as personally. When I left for Washington, D.C., I went with my tail between my legs. Yet each of my mentors stayed with me through that transition, and several surprise parties let me know that there were people who valued what I was able to accomplish in that church unit. But my disillusionment with the church and my cynicism about my fellow ordained clergy were very strong.

If anything restored my faith in the work of the Holy Spirit, it was the place of ministry in which I landed in Washington, D.C. The Metropolitan Ecumenical Training Center (METC) was directed by Tilden Edwards. Even though Tilden was my age, he provided me with a model of how to be a socially aware, yet spiritually authentic, church professional in the midst of a compromising church. Tilden was exactly the kind of mentor I needed in coming off my negative experience with the Lutherans in Pennsylvania. Our job at the center was to provide ways in which the Protestant, Roman Catholic, and Jewish congregations in the Washington area could address the social and political issues of the city. Tilden had successfully led that ministry for ten years. He had returned from a sabbatical leave convinced that there was a need to revitalize the civil rights movement by providing a spiritual base for social justice and political action. We began all our staff meetings with periods of silent meditation. Because his interests were moving elsewhere, he very confidently turned work over to me. At first I could not believe that I was being entrusted with this kind of responsibility. From my former experience I had truly come to believe that I was a socially irresponsible radical who could not be trusted. In the midst of this new work, I felt deeply cared for as an individual. Would that every budding church leader could have such a mentor.

Just as funds for urban training ministries began to dry up all across the country, so they did also in Washington. When METC began to have financial difficulties, I knew I would need to help it along with some outside consultative work. It was just then that The Alban Institute began gaining support for its work and ministry with clergy and congregations. I volunteered to head up the research on clergy changing parishes. In the process I met a fourth important mentor in my training and development—Loren Mead. Loren provided me with a model of how to care deeply for the church even when it was making massive blunders, and how to bring insights from behavioral science to clergy and congregations who were struggling to make their congregations better. Here again, I discovered that a mentor is one who shows you how to pull it all together into personal and professional effectiveness. In Loren I was able to observe someone with high interpersonal skills bringing sound behavioral science theory to bear on practical problems that churches were facing. I learned from him how research can provide people with solid, practical aids, and that research is far more than erudite reports that end up on book shelves, but are of little use to people facing the firing line in parishes on a day-to-day basis.

Loren also taught me how central congregations are to the whole religious enterprise in this country and how to have compassion for the people trying to make those congregational systems work. Looking back on my career in the church, I do not know where I would be if those four mentors had not been there for me precisely at the times I needed them most.

Functions of Support Groups

I also feel blessed at this juncture in my life with the quality of support communities that regularly feed and nurture me and that give my life perspective. I can take some credit for the formation and sustenance of these support communities because I appear to have learned well the need for support for personal and professional effectiveness. Several of these communities have taken hard, intentional work on my part to form and develop. In return for this intentional work, they have given me in great abundance the insight and support I needed to address the issues of my life.

As I review my current support network, I would characterize what these relationships have offered me as follows:

Blankets—There have been times recently when I have felt so broken and vulnerable that I needed people simply to gather around me to protect and hold me. In the presence of the group, I had no need to appear strong and self-sufficient; I could be as vulnerable and insecure as I felt.

Sandpaper—There are times when I am internally locked in nonproductive patterns, and I need someone to give me a swift kick in the pants and tell me to knock it off. There are also times when I am engaged in self-destructive behavior, and I need a group of folks who care enough for me to confront me with this destructiveness.

Authentication—More often than not I find myself wallowing in uncertainty, not knowing if what I'm doing with my life really amounts to a hill of beans. My struggle with certain issues seems to me like straining at gnats. In the midst of this malaise, my support communities often jolt me into realizing that the things I am doing are important and that they have an investment in my seeing them through. They also help me see that I am a worthwhile person, even when there does not seem to be any external evidence that points to this.

Perspective—Place a star by this by-product of a quality support group. It can easily be underemphasized and underappreciated. Yet how much more effective we are as persons when we bring a healthy perspective to a troubled situation.

There is that old saying that everyone has heard yet which presents such a vivid picture of what it is often like trying to be effective in ministry: "It's hard to remember that your task is to drain the swamp when you are up to your ass in alligators." I would add that there is fog on the swamp as well. Few people realize how complex parish ministry can be. It is common for those not fully immersed in parish ministry to have simplistic answers to church problems. Most of the clergy I know, however, are doing the best they can with what they have and are as bewildered as anyone else about why some things work and others don't, and why sheer effort cannot make a church come alive.

In this situation a quality support group can be a great aid, providing somewhere to go to talk about being in the foggy swamp, about trying to find a foothold somewhere, and about not seeing clearly where you are heading, all the while having a handful of church leaders nipping at your backside. After sharing your malaise with a group, one or two comments from these outsiders can be like the sun rising over the swamp and for just a few minutes enabling you to see the whole situation clearly. Eventually the fog will return and you will find yourself lost again, but the prospect of going to a support group meeting and getting a different perspective on the situation makes all the time and effort worthwhile.

Parachute—There are times when my support network helps me see that I am in a lot more trouble than I think I am, and we piece together a parachute that I can use to bail out and land on my feet somewhere else. This is far different from being thrown from the plane and somehow managing to survive the fall; in such cases it can take years for people to struggle back to a place of health. All of us know of clergy who have been thoroughly brutalized by a congregational situation and, lacking a support community, remain permanent casualties of the church.

Rubber Raft—This last symbol applies to us as persons trying to traverse the rapids of an adult life transition. Daniel Levinson informs us that we adults go through a major internal transition about once every ten years. The age forty crisis is usually the most traumatic transition for males in our culture. In such transition periods something begins to change on the inside, and much as we try by sheer will and effort, we cannot get the genie back into the former bottle.

A dramatic example might be a successful thirty-eight-year-old executive who leaves a model home of wife and two kids every day in his pinstripe, three-piece suit and drives his sedan to work. Then suddenly for some strange reason none of this seems to mean anything anymore. At the other end of this transition, we have a divorced male wearing cowboy boots and jeans with a big belt buckle and driving a motorcycle or a convertible. Something changed on the inside, and it probably tore him apart not knowing why he could no longer pump meaning into the former life structure.

This example illustrates the process of life transitions that seem to change our whole perspective on our life situation, our work, our relationships, and ourselves. In the midst of one of these life transitions, it can feel like we are going crazy. What's worse is that often our friends in the former life structure abandon us, or possibly we abandon them because they are not able to support what we are becoming.

Having a support group that sees you through one of these adult life transitions is like someone throwing you a rope when you think you are about to drown in the choppy sea. It is both privilege and pain to see someone through one of these transitions. I have watched and prayed with a group as different members went through such transitions. What a wonder to see the butterfly that emerges at the other end of such a metamorphosis. Even though I went through my age forty crisis on my own (losing both my job and my marriage), I have since experienced several additional adult life crises in which a support group provided me with a rubber raft. In it I was able to traverse some rocky rapids.

The Current State of My Support Network

By delineating the current state of my support network, I hope you may get a glimpse of what some intentional work on this aspect of life can produce. This description includes not only the foundational work in getting support systems started in my life, but also the work I do to maintain the quality of that support.

Marriage

For many persons, the relationship with a marital partner is the most profound support base. That daily diet of touching and care can make a real difference in our lives. The December 4, 1987 edition of *USA Today* carried a study that claimed our chances of surviving cancer are much greater if we are married than if we are single. The researchers found that unmarried people were 23 percent more likely to die from the disease than people who are married.

But all of us know that maintaining a high quality of support within marriage can often be complex and difficult. Each of us is dynamic and thus constantly changing, requiring a constant readjustment of the marital agreement. In a time of marital discord, our prospects of receiving personal and professional support from a marriage may appear elusive indeed.

I believe the relationship my wife Carole and I currently have is on a solid footing. Each of us appears to be getting all the affection and support we need for daily living. I feel lucky to be in a relationship with such a neat, caring person. Having been through a divorce, I have come to realize what a special relationship we have.

Yet there have been many stormy times in this fourteen-year marriage. At times I was not sure we were going to make it. We've had to learn to fight with each other, and fight fairly. We've had some very competent outside help in making this relationship work. Currently we find ourselves checking in periodically (possibly twice a year) with a therapy couple. Bruce and Sheila Barth are qualified psychotherapists. The four of us spend a three-hour block of time together when we take on a marital issue. It's great having both a male and a female perspective as we face our craziness.

Because a healthy marriage can be so central to our well-being, it's important to be intentional about the support given that relationship. What are the relationships and activities that support a healthy marriage? Several years ago, *USA Today* cited a study that correlated the health of marriages with couples having strong friendships outside the marriage. Those conducting the study surmised that having a buddy of the same gender outside the marriage tends to take the heat off those periods in a marriage when things are not working well.

Carole and I are both part of an ongoing support group that meets regularly. We also belong to the same professional organization, the Association for Creative Change. People within these systems have an investment in the quality of our relationship, and thus it is not uncommon for someone to ask, "How are things going with you and Carole?"

Extended Family

Few extended family systems work without a good deal of effort on the part of one or two key members. Without this effort it is too easy for families to drift apart. Members may get together occasionally, but there is a lack of ongoing commitment to each other's lives.

I feel blessed by my extended family support system, but it has meant work and sacrifice on my part. My two older brothers (with five kids each), my two younger sisters (one with four children and one with three), and my mother live in Canada. My brothers live in eastern Canada, while my two sisters and my mother live in western Canada. (This is like having family in New Jersey and Iowa). Yet for the last twenty years, we three brothers and our families have spent Christmas together somewhere in eastern Canada. I have had the privilege of romping with nieces and nephews around the Christmas tree and most recently have been romping with their offspring. My mother alternates Christmases between the eastern and western Oswalds.

The Vietnam War almost did in the positive relationship I have with my bothers. In 1960 I was on the opposite side of the fence from the two of them. Christmas dinner was marked at times by superficial conversation and stifled anger. Conflict about how and when the family ought to celebrate Christmas also nearly did us in. We've had to be flexible and shift our patterns to meet the objections of some.

In the summer of 1990 we held another family reunion in which all of us met at a lake outside Winnipeg, Manitoba. For some people, sacrificing a portion of their vacation to be with aunts, uncles, grandparents, nieces, and nephews is unthinkable. They don't even *like* many members of their extended family, so sacrificing time and money is out of the question. But we are fairly lucky. We generally enjoy one another. Yet we work at deepening our relationships. At this reunion we spent three hours on Sunday evening roasting Freida Oswald's five offspring and their spouses. People had put a lot of time into the songs, skits, and poems that pointed up the mishaps and foibles of these ten people. During the roast we held our sides with laughter and also remembered tender moments. We ended the reunion with a deeper appreciation for one another.

Through the years I have found myself acting as a catalyst for family events that touch a deeper side of life. As the only ordained person in the family, I took it upon myself to play the part of the resident holy man when the spiritual side of our gatherings needed highlighting. In doing this I have developed a profound respect for rituals. I've studied what Emile Durkheim had to say about the power of rituals, and I've become much more aware of their role in religious communities. Yet their role in families can be even more important. Durkheim notes that no matter where one places a Jewish family in the world, it doesn't seem to lose its Jewishness, unlike so many other families from other religions or nationalities. He claims that the old family rituals that are observed in the homes of devout Jews make the difference.

At our Christmas gatherings of the extended family, some things have become as predictable as the snow coming in January to Canada:

— There is always some stollen (sweet fruit bread) and coffee to begin the day.

— There is always a huge Christmas tree.

— We only open gifts when everyone is together and present.

— For at least one hour during the afternoon, one person leads the rest of us in a serious discussion of that person's choosing. (This ritual began twelve years ago with the adults, and we are now having the nieces and nephews take their turns. Subjects have ranged from "Can Computers Feel" to "Marriage versus Just Living Together." Last year one of the nieces talked about the importance of breathing properly and had all of us get down on our hands and knees on the floor to practice abdominal breathing. There was much clowning in the process, but at least the crew of twenty-three adults gave her a hearing.)

—We spend a couple of hours at the end of Christmas singing carols, which never fails to include our dividing into groups of three to rewrite the words to "The Twelve Days of Christmas." Each year's version reflects what is happening to us now as a family.

— We close with a blessing of the babies, when each grandparent gets to hold a grandchild in the center of the circle as the rest of us gather around. When Mother is present she gets to offer the prayers, otherwise, this role is taken by one of the other adults. Everyone is physically touching one of the seven grandchildren during the prayers.

— The singing of "Silent Night" ends the evening.

To be sure, I have had a key role in initiating and supporting these rituals through the years. Yet now, these rituals would carry on without my presence. I believe they have had a strong role in keeping us together as an extended family.

It is my strong belief that all worthwhile support systems have some rituals that help keep them in place.

The Association for Creative Change

The Association for Creative Change (ACC) is an international association of trainers and consultants held together by a steering committee and an annual conference. Our old name used to be the Association of Religion and the Applied Behavioral Scientists (ARABS). We loved that old name, yet felt we had to change it and the accompanying acronym for the sake of our Jewish clientele. I have been a member of ACC for the past fifteen years and have served as president for two terms. There have been many years when I thought about quitting. We have gone through some dry years of uncreative annual conferences. Our membership has fluctuated wildly, and for the past six years we have teetered on the brink of extinction. Yet it is the one organization that year after year brings me back into relationship with many of the people who make their livings in ways similar to mine. I often have difficulty explaining to strangers or even to family members exactly what I do for a living. At ACC most people understand fairly clearly the unique joys and pressures of my work.

ACC offers a special kind of support to its members. It has a professional recognition process that challenges its members to become the best they can be. We can each claim to be professionally competent in specific skill tracks such as Personal Growth, Group Development, Organizational Dynamics, Experiential Education, and Community Organization. Once we have assessed our own skill in those areas, we invite the feedback of other professionals. Once we are recognized as professionally competent in any one of those tracks, we are required to have our skills reviewed every five years. That's a kind of professional accountability I don't find in other associations.

The prime value of ACC to me is its four-day annual conference, held in a different part of the country each year. I have not missed an annual conference in ten years. Twenty to forty workshops are available depending on the theme. It's a place I can go to offer a workshop on a subject that represents a new frontier in my thinking. Yet even when the program isn't very exciting to me, the ACC annual conference is the place where I always get lots of hugs and a chance to be with old friends who live all over this continent. The conference includes some nice long walks with people whose journeys I have shared for years, very stimulating conversations over meals, new ideas growing out of workshops, and dancing every night at a cabaret. This may be the only time during a year when I get out and dance for a couple of hours each night. Once again, the rituals hold us together.

Phrogs

Phrogs is a special group of ACC members who live near the Washington, D.C., area. Membership in Phrogs is by invitation only. The group meets twice a year for an overnight. Anyone missing more than two meetings without letting us know is dropped from the list. We have kept the membership at fifteen to eighteen members. The group meets the first Friday and Saturday each November and the last Friday and Saturday each April. The purpose of Phrogs is providing personal and professional support. The group has been going strong for the past fourteen years. We are not sure where the name came from. At one of our first meetings we were considering a theory by Gerry Harvey entitled "Organizations as Frog Farms." Someone also thought we were forming "For Roy Oswald's Good."

The ritual of Phrogs is fairly well established. We begin on a Friday evening at six for drinks and informal conversation. Following dinner prepared by our hosts, we gather for several hours of personal sharing. Everyone is expected to lay out the highs and lows of their lives since the last time we met. For whatever reasons, the truth telling that takes place on these Friday nights is often quite moving. I have found it a privilege to be so intimately connected with this handful of people over such a long period of time.

The last thing we do Friday evening is a quick inventory of the theories, designs, and problem consultations we have brought with us for group consideration. Our covenant at Phrogs is to share not only the joys and sorrows of our lives, but also the growing edges of our professional lives. We simply go around the circle and place on newsprint what each person is prepared to offer the next day.

At times I have been able to describe some research I'm working with at The Alban Institute, getting the group's reactions and perceptions. At other times, people have put forward a new theory they have been working on and had the group help flesh it out. Occasionally we deal with a war story and have the group debrief the event. On even rarer occasions we find ourselves distressed about what is taking place on the planet and schedule time to talk about our fears and impressions. Yet the basic norm is that we will move from personal issues Friday evening to professional skills and insights on Saturday. The group then makes some choices about the issues on which it wishes to focus from nine to five on Saturday.

The last hour on Saturday is spent on any business issues we need to deal with as a support community, plus a critique of our time together. These critique periods are important because we continually act on ways we can further enrich our life together. I believe that many support groups falter at this point by failing to critique their life together so that improvements can constantly be made. At Phrogs, the ending critique has become a ritual. We simply would find it hard to end without that closing period of reflection.

The other strong ritual at Phrogs is that everyone gets a bear hug when we first meet on Friday evening and when we close on Saturday afternoon.

My Men's Awareness Group

The Men's Awareness Group is the last support group of mine I will describe. Although it began more by accident, once it had begun, the members felt its value and worked to continue it.

I enrolled in the Spiritual Directors Program, sponsored by The Shalem Institute for Spiritual Formation in Washington, D.C. This two-year program required that I have at least two people coming to me specifically for spiritual direction. The program also required that I meet monthly with a group of others who were offering spiritual direction. The group was to guide us as we took on the spiritual issues of those coming to us for direction.

A colleague of mine had been meeting with such a group in Columbia, Maryland. When I approached him about forming a group in the Frederick area, he became enthusiastic about the idea and began to invite others to join us. That first year we had a mixture of men and women who were offering spiritual counsel to others. We talked about our experiences as spiritual directors. Occasionally one of us would ask to record the discussion about one of those we were directing so we could send the tape to Shalem for review and comment.

During the second year the group membership shifted. Four men and one woman attended regularly. One snowy winter day only the four men showed up. Inexplicably, the quality of our meeting that day was different than it had been. Conscious of newfound energy in the group, we decided to meet again as a foursome, two hours prior to our regular meeting. We four men met from ten till noon and then went to lunch together before meeting from one to three with the lone woman. This process went on for several months before we told our female participant what was taking place. She graciously encouraged us to continue to meet as a men's group, and she sought out the support of another group. That was five years ago. Since that time the four of us have been meeting once a month from eleven to three. The sharing has been rich and deep.

Once I had completed the Shalem Spiritual Directors Program, the emphasis of the group shifted to the issues of male spirituality. We knew, at least in theory, that at certain points in the spiritual journey the experience of men differs from that of women. As a group we began trying to see how this was true for us. We keep each other informed about the joys and tribulations of our lives, but the theme of male spirituality is one that uniquely characterizes this support group.

The rituals of the group are rather uncomplicated. We give each other a bear hug at first greeting. Lately we have been starting our group life with a chant that goes on for about five minutes. That is followed by another five minutes of silence. One of the group members then ends the silence with a brief prayer. We then begin our time of personal sharing. A jug of apple cider usually sits at the center of our group. Our time together continues over lunch at a local restaurant and then again back at our place of meeting. We end with a critique of our time together and another bear hug before we depart.

Last year the group hit a crisis when one of our members was elected bishop of a diocese in the Midwest. We had supported Jack throughout the whole election process, and then celebrated with him the victory of his election. At our last meeting as a foursome we took the time to reflect on our history as a support group, highlighting our strengths and shortcomings. Once Jack left, the three remaining members decided to continue to meet as a threesome for at least a year until we became clearer about how we might expand our number. Two of us experienced such transition in our lives that we could not conceive of trying to bring one or two new members in at the time, and we all recognized intuitively that our life as a support group was in jeopardy as we contemplated adding new members. A misjudgment about the addition of one person could spell the end of our trust level and our commitment to giving this group a high priority in our lives. Time will tell whether we will survive this transition into a new support group.

In summary, I am aware of both the rich quality of the support I am feeling in my life right now and the work I have put into developing and sustaining that support network. That network currently has the following components:

- Two formal groups that meet regularly, one monthly and one every six months. I don't think twice about sharing the darker side of my personality with the group that meets monthly. It's the place where "true confession" is standard practice for me.
- One professional association with contacts that range over the course of the last fifteen years. This group helps me remain accountable for what I do professionally. The group also takes professional ethics seriously.
- A strong marriage, with professional support that helps keep it that way.
- An extended family that has evolved as an island of grace after some stormy years.
- Three mentors who continue to provide me with guideposts for the journey ahead.
- An Irish Catholic laywoman who has been my spiritual director for the past eight years. We get together approximately once a month. This is a professional relationship as I pay her a fee each time we meet, yet I experience her as an oasis where I can always return for a graced perspective on my life.
- An adult class in my local congregation that is willing to struggle with Carole and me in the deeper issues of life. At Trinity Lutheran Church in Boonsboro, I also have a real "people-lover" for a pastor.

Joe Dovevan always seems glad to see me when I show up at church, and I can always count on a bear hug from him.
– More friends than I have time to see.

For an introvert, this is a lot of human contact on a regular basis. At times it feels like an overload, and when it does I retreat into a shell for a while. But I've learned the importance of the unique qualities of support I receive from each of the different components of my support network. As I face an uncertain future, personally and professionally, I do so with confidence knowing the quality of the relationships that will be there for me regardless of what trauma or difficulty should hit me. How different life would have been for me had this been true earlier in life.

NOTES

1. Gary L. Harbaugh, William C. Behrens, Jill M. Hudson, and Roy M. Oswald, *Beyond the Boundary* (Washington, DC: The Alban Institute, 1986).

CHAPTER II

Analyzing Your Need for Support

In the last chapter I presented some candid reflections on my own life, from my early days when I desperately needed support and didn't have it, to the present when, after considerable intentional effort, I have a high quality of support surrounding me. Part of the difficulty in my earlier life and ministry was that I was unaware of my need for support and thus did little to develop a support network. Yet I did not possess the skills and insight necessary to analyze the kinds of support I had and the kinds I lacked or know how to improve specific kinds of support that would have made a real difference to me personally and professionally.

In this chapter I will present some ways you can reflect on areas of your life in which the quality of support is low, thus allowing you to become more intentional about improving the support in those areas.

To begin, I want to tell you about some research that has correlated support with certain aspects of living.

I am especially intrigued by the research of Eric Lindemann, who interviewed the survivors of the Cocoanut Grove fire in which 129 people were killed. He discovered that there were basically two kinds of survivors. One group of survivors recovered quickly from the disaster, and for some of them their level of well-being was higher after the fire than before. These people had a high quality of support throughout their period of trauma. From Lindemann's point of view, this support did not consist of in-depth therapy or counseling. It had more to do with the number of people who checked on that individual over a period of time. If a person had a significant number of others checking just to see how they were or simply to listen to them, Lindemann considered their quality of support high. He was also impressed with the speed of their recovery and their high level of self-esteem following this traumatic occurrence.

In contrast, those who did not have that kind of support system had a long and painful recovery. Lindemann also discovered that very rarely did they recover the level of well-being they experienced before the tragedy.

The study illustrates the dramatic difference a support network can make in the lives of people confronted by a trauma or tragedy. It highlights for me what basic human contact can do for people who believe they are in a crisis. At this point some congregations are at their best. This is certainly not true for all congregations, but in some congregations a lot of people are going to find ways to "touch" you when you are in a crisis. Although some of the human contact may seem superficial, it's amazing what it can do to heal a torn psyche.

I am also interested in the research of Anton Antonovsky, an Israeli professor who teaches medical sociology at Ben Gurion University. Antonovsky cites a nine-year study of 7,000 people in Alameda County, California. The study shows that people with many social ties (such as marriage, close friendships, extended families, church membership, and other group associations) have far lower mortality rates. These data are supported by the work of Antonovsky's associate Lisa Berkman, an epidemiologist at Yale University. She found that men in their fifties who seemed to be at high risk because of very low social and economic status, but who scored high on an index of social networks, lived far longer than high status men with low social network scores.

Antonovsky goes on to point out that in extreme cases the loss of one's social ties can even kill. He points to the phenomenon of voodoo death among tribes in Australia, Central Africa, and the Caribbean. When an individual in one of these primitive tribes breaks a tribal taboo and the tribe decides to punish that person, the witch doctor points a magic bone at him and recites some incantations that place him under a spell of death. Those of you who have read the novel *Clan of the Cave Bear* by Jean Auel will recognize the ceremony as it was conducted on Ayla. Harvard psychologist Walter Cannon quotes the account of an Australian explorer as he describes the results of the voodoo rite:

> The man who discovers that he is being "boned" is a pitiable sight.
> He sways backwards and falls to the ground. He writhes as if in
> mortal agony, and covering his face with his hands begins to moan.
> After a while, he becomes very composed and crawls into his

worley [hut]. From this time onward, he sickens and frets. His
death is only a matter of comparatively short time.

In Cannon's view, the primary factor in the victim's disintegration is
the withdrawal of tribal support. Once the bone is pointed, his fellow
tribesmen give him up as dead, and in his isolation he has no alternative
but to die. His heart becomes exhausted by overstimulation, his blood
pressure drops calamitously, and his vital functions cease. In *Clan of
the Cave Bear*, Auel describes Ayla's experience of having all the people
in the clan look beyond her as if she weren't there and begin living as
though she didn't exist. Persons in primitive societies are usually much
more embedded in their social group.

It is hard for us in the 20th century to imagine that someone would
die if people withdrew their support from him or her. This is simply
because we live in such a complex interaction of social networks that if
we are "boned" by one group of people, we have four or five other communities to which we can turn for support. If, however, we lived in a
society in which a single community was our whole world and that community withdrew its support, I believe none of us would live very long
either. Studies have indicated that young babies die soon after birth if
they are not loved into life. Similarly, studies in Russia correlate illness
and death with extreme cases of loneliness. The need for support is that
basic to human life: without it, we die.

If support is so essential to human life, it certainly must be essential
to professional competence and well-being. I believe that parish clergy
are particularly vulnerable within certain congregations. We all know
that some congregations are "clergy-killers." These are congregations
that learn to solve problems by firing clergy. Rather than looking at
some of the deeper reasons why their parish is malfunctioning, they find
it easier and safer to scapegoat clergy. For clergy to make it politically
in any congregation, they need to be viewed positively by members of
that congregation, or at least by a critical mass (whatever that number
might be) within the congregation. Yet in order to assist congregations
in growing, clergy at times need to take unpopular stands in the parish.
This is an important aspect of leadership. When clergy underestimate the
depth of disfavor a certain change is going to elicit from the congregation, they often find themselves out of sync with a large segment of the
parish. Depending on the depth of people's anger toward the pastor,

members of the congregation may try to "bone" the pastor. They begin to wish that the pastor no longer existed in their midst.

Typically, our ordination as clergy occurs when our denomination puts its stamp of approval on us through the service of the "laying on of hands." Yet we can also view ordination as taking place at another level, when a congregation calls us to be pastor, to be their resident holy person. It is often frightening to see how quickly certain members of a congregation can try to unordain clergy. Essentially they live as though the pastor is no longer qualified to be their personal religious authority. In these situations, clergy only survive when there is another critical mass of people who are behind them and who affirm their ordination, their right to exercise ministry in that place. I am continually struck by the fact that a clergyperson's career path depends so heavily on succeeding with a small community. In other words, the economic and psychological well-being of clergy depends on their remaining popular with a small cadre of people.

Related to this is my observation that women are still not supported in the church when they assume ordination. To be sure, women have won some major battles, and the ordination of women is now taken for granted in most mainline Protestant churches. Yet the statistics indicate that support for the ministry of clergywomen in the church is still marginal. These days most Protestant seminaries have student bodies that are nearly fifty percent women, some have even exceeded that figure. Those women will be ordained and the church will somehow find entry-level positions for them.

Yet look at the statistics on the percentage of clergywomen in your denomination. For most denominations this figure is still below fifteen percent. A huge fallout occurs because these women are either kept at entry-level positions or have so many negative experiences that they quit. This is one of the reasons why there are so few female mentors for newly ordained clergywomen. The number of clergywomen with ten to fifteen years of parish experience is still relatively small. Thus, even though we claim to support the ministry of clergywomen in our church systems, in other ways those women are still being "boned."

In many ways most of us, men and women alike, pursued our dreams of becoming parish pastors in a naive fashion. When we made the decision to dedicate our lives to God in service of God's people in parish systems, little did we know how vulnerable we would be to the withdrawal of support from parish members. We are just here to serve God. Why would anyone want to kill us? Yet in many ways we are being killed, and we couldn't be killed by a nicer group of people. For the most part the average church member is not mean or malicious; most of them are also unconscious of their role in "boning" a pastor. In the voodoo deaths of those primitive tribes, the persons within the tribe would respond in utter disbelief if told that they participated in the death of the boned person. From their point of view, the magic of the ritual killed the person; they were innocent bystanders, unaware of how they withdrew their support and no longer saw that person as being alive. Yet when they withdrew their support from the victim it was as though each one had stuck a knife into the boned person's heart.

Yet congregations are not completely unaware that they occasionally "bone" their pastors in a similar way and use him or her as a scapegoat for their own darker side. At an unconscious level they conclude that "it is expedient that one man should die for the sake of the people" (John 18:14). Parishioners generally allow this to happen through inaction and passivity.

That clergy are trained to hide their difficulties doesn't help. Clergy passivity at difficult times is not at all helpful. Yet I have seen clergy in crisis situations stand by passively, certain that someone from the congregation will come to their side to rescue them.

Thus, in The Alban Institute's "Clergy in Transition" seminars, we emphasize the notion of building a support system within the parish before initiating any changes. Our rule of thumb is that for the first nine to twelve months in a new parish the primary role of the incoming pastor is to be a lover and a historian. This involves finding something to love in everyone in the parish and finding out how this parish has functioned in the past, especially with former clergy. Only after a year of building a support base, especially with the power people in the parish, can one move on to becoming a change agent. Even with this advice, many clergy cannot refrain from moving in and making changes before they have scoped out the land. Tragically, many of these changes are more cosmetic and matters of personal taste than they are changes of substance that might ensure the greater health of the parish. Yet the price paid in making the change remains the same.

If we had been trained as community organizers, our training would teach us to build our support in a new community before trying any type of change action. As it is, most of us in parish ministry simply dive into our work, expecting support to be forthcoming, if we are authentic and have good intentions.

To remain effective within a congregation, we as parish clergy must function with a high degree of support from within the parish and outside that system. Little of significance will happen inside a parish without a high degree of support there. Yet effectiveness will also be proportional to the quality of support we have outside our congregations. We need that support for our health and self-esteem. We also need it for perspective. Being able to stand outside our congregations and view those systems at a distance with some knowledgeable people can greatly enhance our ability to productively reengage those congregations.

I hope you have found the concept of "boning" helpful in giving you some insight into the quality of support you have within the systems where you do ministry. I would now like to return to the implications of the research discussed and ask you to reflect more deeply on the support you need as an individual, outside of a role. As Lindemann, Antonovsky, and Berkman indicate, your ability to endure crisis as well as your ability to live a long and healthy life depend upon the quality of your personal support network. Being effective in ministry depends as much on who you are as a person and your health and vitality as it does upon your skill and knowledge. Whatever you do to enhance your personal wholeness will proportionally enhance your ministry. Yet personal wholeness is not possible without support, hence the need to seek support for yourself as well as for your active ministry.

Support Analysis Exercise

I would now like to engage you in an exercise that should lead to a fuller grasp of the height, depth, and breadth of your personal support. To derive the most value from this exercise, put down this book for three or four minutes. Make a list of all the people you would classify as your "encouragers." These are people who believe in you, value what you are trying to accomplish, and have an investment in your well-being. These are people who help you feel good about yourself, and whenever you are with them your self-esteem increases.

Please take a few minutes now and make as long a list as you can of your personal "encouragers."

Good! Now lets work with that list to see what kind of depth and breadth it has.

Draw a circle around the names of at least three people on that list, other than members of your immediate family (spouse, parents, children, in-laws, brothers or sisters) who, in the event of a crisis in your life (such as a broken back or the death of a spouse) would drop what they were doing and come to spend several days with you.

Having identified those people, ask yourself, Have I been in personal contact with those people in the past thirty days? How many times in the past thirty days have I initiated contact with these people?

This initial step should help you become aware of two things. First, do you have people engaged in your life other than your immediate family who would make major sacrifices for you in a time of your need? Second, what kind of a supporter are you? Are you someone who demands support from others, but who does not consistently take the initiative to support others?

Next draw a line through the names of four groups of people on your list.

The first group of people to take off your list are members of your immediate family (spouse, parents, children, brothers or sisters). One reason for temporarily drawing a line through those names is that, according to research, we clergy tend to overuse our families. More than people in any other profession, we bring our problems home with us and unload them on our families. Possibly one reason for this is that we have so few places where we can go to talk candidly about what is happening to us within our parish. In addition to overburdening our families with all those problems, we show them a side of the church that no one else sees. Yet they are unable to do much about it, which is hardly fair to them. This burdening and impotence may account for the alienation of many clergy spouses from the church. When we come home ranting and raving about Joe Schmutt did to us at the last session meeting, guess who else begins to see Joe Schmutt as a demonic person? Months later we may become reconciled with Joe Schmutt. Yet guess who still remains alienated from him? I am no longer surprised at clergy conferences to which spouses are invited to discover that the burnout scores of the spouses are consistently higher than those of clergy themselves. We have got to find places other than our families where we can unload our negativity about the church.

Drawing a line through the names of members of our family prompts us to ask why we have not found places of support outside our family.

The second group of people to take off the list are all those who live more than fifty miles from us. In certain western states we could extend this to 100 miles. Research indicates that we tend to rely less on those support persons who live further away. Whenever we want to be in contact with them we either have to telephone long distance or get into the car and drive for an hour or more. When we are down and depressed, driving for an hour to reach a friend may take more effort than we can manage. It's much easier to go to bed or stare at the tube. And when telephone bills are a little high, we think twice about calling someone long distance and talking for an hour.

Drawing a line through these people also prompts us to ask why we have not developed support persons closer to home.

The third group of people to take off the list are all members of your denomination. In workshops, removing this third group generally wipes out the lists of many people, meaning they are simply not relating to people outside their denominational systems.

Why is it so bad to have all your support within your denomination? Because to do so makes you vulnerable. There is no guarantee that you will be able to remain an ordained minister within your denomination. Who would support you if you had to leave the parish ministry for some reason or another? When I left my job with the Lutherans in Pennsylvania and moved into ecumenical work, I lost all my Lutheran support. It was not that my friends in that system abandoned me. Essentially, I abandoned them. Because we did not travel in the same circles, we lost touch. I still maintain some contact with people in that system, but it takes real effort and becomes harder and harder as time passes.

The last people to take off your list are all ordained or full-time church workers from other denominations. As clergy we can easily get caught in a cycle of relationships that lock us into constantly thinking about the church. Besides, as clergy we tend to think alike, and there are times in our lives when we need a lay perspective. We also need to relate to people who have little to do with the church and who do not relate to us as ordained or full-time church workers. We often have difficulty finding places where we can get out of role and be seen as ordinary human beings rather than as people symbolizing religion.

Do you still have anyone on your list? If you do, you have probably put some real effort into maintaining those relationships. The more people you have left on your list, the greater the breadth of your support network.

Please do not think you need to abandon the people on your list who have lines drawn through their names. Be thankful for those people as well. This exercise has a twofold purpose. First, it will show you how blessed you are by being in relationship with some quality people. Have you been openly appreciative of them, letting them know specifically what you appreciate about them and what they do for you? Second the exercise will heighten your awareness of where your personal support network is a little soft and where you could be more intentional about improving the kind of support you need to be a healthier, more whole person.

Take just a few more minutes to work with your list of encouragers to see whether some ideas may occur to you about how you could choose to raise the quality of personal support in your life.

As you review your list, are there one or two names that should be removed because they do not represent the kind of support you need now? It is easy to get locked into long-term relationships, even when they are toxic to our lives. Each time we are with those people we slip back into destructive patterns. Each time we are with them we end up not feeling so good about ourselves. If nothing more than guilt is keeping us in certain relationships, maybe it's time to kick those people out of our support network. This does not mean you should abandon them in terms of pastoral care. You can find other ways to care for them, but they should not be part of your primary support network.

To be more intentional about building a quality support network for ourselves, we need to clean house from time to time. We also do this to make room for new people in our support network. Because our life goals are constantly changing, we need to invite people who represent growth and change for us into our support system. We return to the basic premise that the healthier we become as individuals—spiritually, emotionally, physically—the more effective we become as spiritual mentors for others.

With every destructive habit in our lives, a wall of resistance within ourselves and within others keeps us locked in place. To get through this wall, we need people who will support the desired change in our lives. In pursuing our journey to wholeness, we must confront our addictions one at a time and thus become less dependent. But there is no way we can confront any addiction, even a minor one, without a lot of support. Who are the people with an investment in our overcoming our addictions? Some of our friends have an investment in our staying just the way we are. We are part of their familiar, predictable environment. If we change, it upsets them. They may feel threatened by our ability to change an aspect of our lives. Our changing becomes a sort of judgment on their inability to get their own destructive patterns more under control. Are there people who are more interested in your remaining the same than changing?

I suspect that every one of us has people on the periphery of our lives who would love to be part of our more intimate support network. We need only to find a way to bring them in closer and to ask them to become invested in some aspect of our lives. Are you able to jot down the names of one or two people who, if they could be included in your more intimate circle of relationships, would make a significant difference in your life? Is it totally out of the question to ask them to come closer into the orbit of your life? What could you contribute to them and their sense of well-being?

Let's keep working on your list.

Are you currently engaged with people who

— Level with you?
— Care enough to hold you accountable?
— Let you be real?
— Ask you difficult questions?
— Enjoy you?
— Give you a sense of your own worth and integrity?
— Help you live with the pain of being different, alone, isolated?
— Affirm that you are competent while allowing you to ask for help?
— Call forth the best that is in you, evoking your gifts?

The answers to those questions may give you some idea of the kind of people you need to round out your support network.

One last piece of analysis before we leave this chapter. This has to
do with the balance between being neither overdependent nor counterdependent. Few people are able to live their lives right in the middle
between those two extremes. We tend either to be more of a "clinging"
person, becoming overdependent upon others, or an "avoiding" person,
rejecting the support of others. On a rating scale between these two
descriptions, where would you place yourself?

1   2   3   4   5   6   7   8   9   10
Overdependent   Counterdependent

Either extreme can make for difficulty in being able to use personal
or work-related social systems effectively. Overdependent people can
either drain a healthy support system or attract domineering types who
tend to take over their lives. Overdependent people lack the self-reliance
to work comfortably and naturally in relationships with other people or
alone.

Counterdependent people tend to go it alone when the help or support of others could make life a whole lot easier for them, and more productive as well.

I have had to struggle with counterdependence for much of my life.
I'm your classic loner. In certain circumstances I can be naive and overdependent upon the perspective of others, yet when I begin to see the
folly of that I break things off and go back to being the loner. Knowing
this has helped me remain more receptive to supportive relationships for
longer periods of time.

Enough analysis. I hope you have gotten some ideas on how you
could productively build support in the years ahead. Now I'd like to tell
you about the research that underlies a new model for developing a
workable peer support system. I conducted this research in Carlisle
Presbytery, a middle judicatory of the Presbyterian Church in central
Pennsylvania.

For the most part, clergy groups do not work. Few deliver the support clergy need in tough ministries. Leadership and trust are key factors
for success or failure. The model I will recommend takes both of those
elements seriously, resulting in groups that tend to work well over time.
Yet unless a few key issues are dealt with, these groups will go the way
of most clergy groups that are little more than "bitch and brag" sessions.

CHAPTER III

The Carlisle Project:
Clergy Morale and Support*

Every second Monday morning at 8:00 a.m., seven people gather for an hour and a half to share important personal and professional issues and then move into silence and prayer. The group gathers at a location within Carlisle Presbytery, a middle judicatory of the Presbyterian Church in central Pennsylvania. It is an ecumenical group, though mostly Presbyterian—four women and three men. Two are not ordained. The major objective of the group is fostering a deeper awareness of the Spirit's movement in the lives of members and providing support for the disciplines of prayer. The basic format begins with each person making a personal statement about what is going on in his or her life at the time. These statements usually lead naturally into the prayer time that follows. The group then moves to silence. A few minutes of shared prayer end the time together.

In another part of Carlisle Presbytery, six young male clergy and a group facilitator meet at Boscov's Restaurant every second Tuesday for lunch. The group laughs a lot, and their humor can be distracting at times. Yet when all have their lunch in front of them, Charlie, the group facilitator, asks each person to take some time to talk about what's going on in his life. The men talk mainly about issues they are confronting in their parishes, although at times personal concerns predominate. One of the members has a brain tumor that will make it necessary for him to leave the ministry. The group has been a major support to him.

Another group of clergy in the presbytery, who serve congregations affected by tourism in the Gettysburg-Chambersburg valley, meets for

---

*This chapter reflects my observations and conclusions about the Carlise Project in 1989.

two hours every month. They rotate their meeting place so they can experience the context of each person's ministry. Chuck Jessen is clearly the facilitator. He sends notices prior to every meeting and makes sure someone has a planned devotional to begin their meetings. He also suggests ways in which the group can foster self-disclosure and discussion of personal and professional issues.

For the past seven years a group of veteran clergy from larger congregations of the presbytery have met every other week in Charlie Idler's office for an hour and a half. They met weekly when one of their members was in a crisis. Several claim the group has saved their ministries more than once. Issues are personal and professional. When they meet they observe a ritual in which each in turn makes a personal statement about their life. They claim they don't need a group facilitator. This pattern has worked for them for a year, however, an observer can see that it is usually Charlie who gently guides them through the process or through any decisions they need to make.

Within the same presbytery, five clergy from inner city ministries meet every second week in a convenient church parlor. Their facilitator, Fred Widman, serves as a chaplain at the local prison. He provides a laid back leadership style. The group members share similar values and problems and continue to find meaning in their meetings. One of the pastors has been forced out of his congregation yet he still meets with the group and finds personal support by doing so.

Once a month, four Presbyterian couples in the western section of the presbytery get together on Friday nights for dinner and conversation. The group is made up mainly of younger clergy couples with small children. The children are included in the monthly gathering. The wives are the main movers behind the gatherings. They prepare the food and arrange for future meetings. During the summer months the group meets for a picnic and an overnight camping trip. Formal discussions are rare; most of the significant conversations take place in smaller groups. The group appears to address one major problem for these couples, namely their social and intellectual isolation from the rest of their congregations.

Four of these six clergy support groups were a result of special effort by a study group in the presbytery established to raise the morale of the clergy. The Alban Institute was asked to assist the study group, and funding was provided by a special grant from someone in the presby-

tery. The primary goal of the project was to improve the total effectiveness of congregations in the presbytery. Clergy revitalization was
seen as one of the best ways to accomplish that goal. Specifically, the
18-month project sought "to revitalize the clergy of the Presbytery of
Carlisle through a project that would focus on their personal health and
professional skills."

The project committee outlined three basic assumptions:

1. Congregational health is correlated with clergy health.
2. We can affect clergy health through developing better support
   systems.
3. Providing dependable leadership for support groups is essential.

The committee recognized that progress toward achieving their
goals would be hard to measure, but the group decided to proceed
anyway. They wanted to do something concrete to address the malaise
felt by many clergy over declining membership in their churches and a
general feeling of discouragement. A large percentage of the clergy
tested high on the Clergy Burnout Inventory. Marital crises and substance abuse were two other symptoms of low clergy morale. Difficulties with professional mobility and the clergy's resultant feeling of being
stuck also contributed to the negative energy in the presbytery.

Spearheading the effort to turn this situation around was Dorothy
Yingling, a retired businesswoman who made her business acumen and
compassion available to church leaders. As chair of the Committee on
Ministry for the presbytery for several years, she had worked at bettering
the lot of clergy in that judicatory. She personally visited all the clergy
in the presbytery twice to garner insight on the special pressures and
problems felt by clergy and their spouses. These visits won her their
respect and trust. She also came to appreciate more fully the complexity
of the clergy role and the particular stresses that afflict many of these
professionals. She was dismayed at the number of burned-out individuals whose marriages were in trouble. Soon, Dottie became the trusted
person in the system to whom the clergy turned to share their plight.

When Dottie's term with the Committee on Ministry ended, she
continued her efforts by facilitating the Carlisle Project and initiating
collaboration with The Alban Institute. She also continued to work
closely with the succeeding chairs of the Committee on Ministry, Bill

Murphy and Jim Tice, in structuring and executing the study. It was clear from the beginning that the study needed the support of the Committee on Ministry, it would also need to be independent of that committee. Legislated solutions to clergy morale issues usually don't work, nor do official actions that form clergy support groups.

After reviewing a variety of strategies for addressing clergy morale and facilitating clergy support groups, the project team decided to begin the process with a two-day clergy retreat. All clergy in the presbytery were invited to the overnight retreat; half attended. As retreat facilitator, I outlined the ways in which stress and burnout bring pressure to bear on clergy. Each participant was administered the Clergy Life Changes Inventory, the Strain Response Inventory, and the Clergy Burnout Survey. With emphasis on pursuing greater self-care, the issue of support communities as a self-care strategy was introduced. We then explored the variety of obstacles to effective clergy support groups, and I outlined the difficulties and complexities in establishing quality support groups:

— We as clergy are mostly trained and conditioned to be lone rangers. We are more adept at giving help than receiving it. We have difficulty asking for what we need from others to sustain our own health.

— As outlined by Robert Bellah in *Habits of the Heart*,[1] a war between individualism and commitment is going on inside us here in North America. We all want support yet fear our individuality might be diminished. The model of strength for our culture is that of rugged individualism as personified in characters like the cowboy or the detective. These individuals give of themselves selflessly in heroic effort while remaining autonomous at the fringe of society. Large numbers of clergy and laity see the effective pastor as playing a similar role. Generally, this is more true of men than of women; the need for support and more collegial skills is greater among clergymen than clergywomen.

— Clergy often feel competitiveness and distrust. If our pastorates are in the same region, we believe we are competing in the same market for the loyalty and support of lay resources. We feel envious when a neighboring pastor launches a new program that results in a spurt of new members. On the other hand, we are loath to give attention to colleagues who are obviously incompetent or who are on self-destructive paths. We deal with so many problem people in our ministries that we have little energy left for our peers.

— The plain hard work of developing trust is a prelude to helpful, supportive relationships. Scott Peck, in his book *A Different Drum*,[2] outlines the struggle that groups must go through before they reach a sense of real community. He outlines the process of group formation as

> Pseudo-community
> Chaos
> Emptiness
> Community

When new communities form, everyone is nice and courteous to each other during the honeymoon phase. Our facades are in place and we try to present the best sides of ourselves. We may swallow our hurts and indignities to keep up the pretense that we feel fine about what is happening in the group. Our dark side, or shadow self, is well hidden or denied. This phase is called Pseudo-community because superficiality is prevalent. When we tire of this and let the facade slip away, more of our true self, along with that of others, emerges. This usually results in Chaos.

The Chaos phase is that time in a group's life when all members are finally candid about their agendas and how they think a group ought to function, and, thus, they run into conflict with each other's agenda for the group. Much of this relates to differences in type, temperament, life-style, theology, age, culture, and background. We don't view support and the nature of ministry in the same way. There is a strength in this, although it must be worked out.

The Emptiness phase is that time of growing maturity when people surrender their agendas and accept people and pro-

cesses for what they are. When this type of surrender is shared
by the rest of the group, Community with richness and depth can
form. It usually differs from what any one of the group members
anticipated, but each member comes to value it.

The process that Scott Peck describes involves courage, risk,
and hard work. Most of us are aware of the difficulty groups
often endure before the level of trust is high enough to share pain
and vulnerability. In our exhaustion or burnout, we are not sure
we have the energy to exert that much effort before we start
getting the support we need for a healthier life. As a result,
many of us muddle through in isolation and loneliness because
creating a good support group seems like too much work. Even
with hard work, there are no guarantees that the group will
emerge with a strength that can add something positive to our
lives.

— The lack of leadership at the center of most groups causes them
to fail. Generally, unless support groups have strong leadership
that facilitates their group process, they will have difficulty
developing the trust that is a prerequisite for self-disclosure and
vulnerability.

— Finally, another impediment to quality support groups is the assumption that support happens by accident; all we need to do is
dive into our work, do our best, and support will be forthcoming. Developing a quality support system for oneself is not a
skill taught either at home or in college. Yet having an effective
support system for personal and professional health requires
learning a variety of skills and hard, intentional work. When we
assume that support happens by accident, we will fail to exert
the effort needed for quality support.

The advantages of peer support groups were also outlined at this
retreat. Given the complexities of the pastoral role, professional support
can come only from peers in ministry. When clergy say they have put in
an eighty-hour week, the average lay person has little idea of what would
consume eighty hours of work in the pastorate. A lay person would
probably interpret it as ineffective time management or just plain incom-

petence. This is because ninety percent of what clergy do is invisible to ninety percent of the lay people ninety percent of the time. When talking with peers in ministry, fellow clergy are well aware of how easy it is to pile up an eighty-hour week. If you have a busy week scheduled and someone dies, you have to add fifteen hours to your week. Two funerals can easily push you into an eighty-hour week.

Understanding the complexities of the role of religious authority is one of the key advantages of a peer support group for clergy. Generally, the three highest contributors to stress for clergy are role ambiguity, role conflict, and role overload. Role ambiguity occurs when we clergy do not have within ourselves a road map about what it means to be a resident religious authority. That ambiguity catapults us into overextending ourselves in the role. Stress technology says that the more ambiguous your role, the higher your stress level. Role conflict occurs when two or more people or groups come to us with conflicting expectations; each thinks we ought to have a set of priorities different than the ones we are pursuing. Role overload occurs when we finally hear everyone out and discover how impossible it would be to fulfill everyone's expectations of us.

A peer support group has one of the best chances of helping us figure out how we might best respond to these role tensions. A peer group can often give us the perspective we need to take charge of our lives once again and move back into our systems, knowing how we are going to resolve some of these role tensions.

Support is also a key component in coping with stress or burnout. One of the reasons clergy burn out is that their lives are no longer in their control. Other people are writing the agenda. To wrest back that control, clergy need support. Some people are going to be unhappy with us because we no longer fulfill their expectations. Before we decided to change, we were part of their predictable environment. In the face of unhappy opposition, few of us are able to stand firm without people behind us. Most of us underestimate our vul-nerability and fold in the face of opposition, reverting to self-destructive patterns.

Thus, our general effectiveness in ministry is directly proportional to the quality of support we have in our lives, and we require a variety of support systems to be competent at our work. We need support within our congregations. Without it, leadership is not possible. We also need support from persons outside our congregations. They bring a distance and objectivity that we lack. An evaluation of our ministry needs to include perspectives from within our systems and from without.

Yet, at the top of the list of advantages of peer support groups is the issue of morale. It is easy to get discouraged in parish ministry. People do not come to church thinking of ways they can take better care of their pastor. They come with their own burdens, wanting attention and nurturing. In congregations with conflict or tension, the blame for the conflict is often laid at the feet of clergy. If the church is not growing the way some lay leaders think it should, they usually put pressure on the clergy to change things. If a presbytery is having budget difficulties or facing internal problems, little caring attention is available to despondent clergy. Instead, presbytery leaders place subtle pressure on clergy to give more, to do more. Committees on Ministry are often so geared to problems in the presbytery that they intervene in a parish only when there is a crisis. By the time the Committee on Ministry is called in, the situation has usually degenerated so badly that clergy are asked to leave. A generalization borne out of experience is that, whenever the Committee on Ministry is called into a parish, the pastor will be resigning within six months. Little wonder that clergy do not feel supported by their judicatory or those in administrative roles, and are therefore forced to deal with their morale issues as best they can on their own. The value of a peer group of trusted clergy is obvious.

In addition to exploring needed steps for maintaining physical, emotional, and spiritual health and analyzing the benefits and difficulties in quality support groups, retreat participants did some preliminary sorting for potential peer support groups. Without committing themselves, people were asked to mill around and congregate with persons with whom they might like to explore the possibility of an ongoing support group. There was some tension in the room as the exercise began. Participants wondered whether they would find themselves locked into groups that were not of their liking, or whether they would be rejected by their peers in such a group selection. For over an hour people walked back and forth between different parts of the room. As the various groups began to cluster, peace seemed to settle on the community. Many clergy were not at the retreat, some had schedule conflicts and some simply chose not to attend. The groups that began forming were free to consider inviting those not at the retreat to be part of their peer group. By the time we moved to closing rituals, six groups had begun to form with possibly two more hinging on some phone calls. Whether or not they would jell would take time to discover.

The retreat took place in October. Some groups began meeting immediately afterward. Others did not get underway until the first of the year. In March we called an all-day meeting of the group facilitators to assess the situation. To our amazement, six groups were already operating. Two had been functioning prior to the retreat. The majority of clergy in the presbytery were in one type of support group or another.

As we listened to each facilitator describe the nature and functioning of their group, we were intrigued at the unique persona each group had assumed. The day provided support, encouragement, direction, and help with problem solving for the facilitators. All agreed to convene a two-hour meeting of their groups with me during the last week in May. My visits were for data gathering and evaluation. In fact, I visited each group twice, six months apart. At the end of eighteen months, six groups continued to meet on a regular basis, some of them throughout the summer months. In the spring of 1989, the project team met to critique the process and form two additional groups to include clergy who were not part of any ongoing support group.

Group Facilitators

In planning this project, we believed that group facilitators were the cornerstone of a healthy group. Without strong leadership, we felt the group would not get off the ground.

The project committee was prepared with the names of several facilitators for each group. The group leaders needed three key characteristics: competence, sensitivity, and safety.

Competence—Facilitators must ensure a process whereby colleagues can move quickly to depth, sharing the key things that are troubling them. Facilitators must possess the skills necessary to man-age whatever difficulties might impede group development. When tension or conflict arises, these facilitators must know how to surface the issues and deal with them directly.

Sensitivity—Facilitators must be sensitive to the unique complexities of pastoral ministry. Sometimes skilled lay persons may not work well because they may not fully understand the special pressures clergy are under. Generally we recommend that the facilitator have some parish experience.

Safety—Facilitators must be safe to be with. The facilitator should not be in a position to influence the career of the clergy involved. Thus some denominational figures do not make good facilitators. If the facilitator is someone the participants need or want to impress, they will always try to put their best foot forward, rather than reveal pain and vulnerability. The group then quickly degenerates into the usual "bitch and brag" sessions that characterize many clergy gatherings.

We at The Alban Institute have observed that when a clergy group has at its center a facilitator who possesses those three qualities, the group is much more likely to move quickly to trust. This is especially true at the beginning of a group's formation. Some clergy groups do not have this type of leadership at their center. When we learn of their history, however, we discover that the initial chemistry was right, and that they made it through the tenuous beginning period with developing trust. Such groups then developed a ritual process that requires little leadership. Additionally, the group's norms (unwritten rules that govern behavior in a group) were healthy enough to deal with inevitable tension or conflict. But I must repeat a simple fact: Most clergy support groups *don't* work. They fail to form enough trust so that pain and vulnerability can be revealed. The key ingredient missing is leadership.

In the Carlisle Project, three of the four new groups had clearly designated leadership. In the case of the younger group of male clergy that met over lunch at Boscov's, a seasoned clergyman in the presbytery volunteered (or was volunteered by Jim Tice, who knew of his competence) to facilitate the group. As I talked with Charlie, it was clear that the group relied on him to keep the process moving and to deal with problems as they arose. Because the group was not a support system for him, we talked about his getting his own needs for support met elsewhere.

In the Gettysburg-Chambersburg group, Chuck Jesson offered his leadership. When I attended these meetings I had no question about who was managing the process. At the end of each meeting Chuck made sure that the group had made the decisions needed for future meetings. More important, he ensured that everyone had some group time, and that the group did not get sidetracked.

In the inner city group the designated facilitator, Fred Widman, was probably a little too laid back when the group began, and it appeared to be floundering. By my second visit, however, Fred was asserting somewhat stronger leadership, and the group was faring better.

In the fourth group, which addressed the spiritual quest, two persons were identified as giving informal leadership to the group—Rebecca Langer and Paul Derrickson. I observed that it was Rebecca who tended to keep the group process moving, but when I asked the group if they had a leader, they were unsure. They thought they followed a similar process each time they met and therefore didn't need a leader. When I asked Rebecca what the informal leadership she provided the group was costing her (including ease of participation), she claimed it was a lot. The group seemed surprised to hear that Rebecca's leadership role sometimes detracted from her ability to be a participant and receive from the group.

This may seem like a minor point, but I believe its importance is often overlooked by support groups. When I hear of clergy groups that seem to function well without a designated leader, I usually ask how they make decisions or what happens when the group gets hung up or sidetracked. Inevitably one name surfaces as the person the group turns to in such circumstances. Both the group and the informal leader may be unaware that the quality of support experienced by that one individual may be diminished. In fact, this clergy person is making a considerable sacrifice for the sake of the group's life and health. When I explain the theory of extradependence, someone who has been having a clergy group meet in his office for years says, "Yes, I think I really did that for the group, and I don't think I was fully appreciated for that sacrifice." I therefore still believe strongly that it is more helpful to specify the leadership role consciously and directly. Group members should make a contract for the leadership that is needed for group trust and health and pay for it if necessary.

The group of veteran clergy from larger parishes claimed they didn't have a leader, but I noticed that Charlie was the one who kept things on track. In the clergy couples group that met for dinner once a month, Eileen Best, the wife of the local Presbyterian minister, held the group together.

Why the strong emphasis on leadership? The Grubb Theory of

Oscillation is one explanation. The theory was first developed by Bruce Reed of the Grubb Institute in London. Reed drew heavily on Victor Turner's study of primitive religions around the world and the research of Wilfred Bion on the unconscious forces at work in group behavior.

The theory describes two modes of life between which we oscillate.

Doing
Meeting the requirements of an achievement oriented culture.

Being
Accepting who and what we are.

Work
Energy expended toward the accomplishments of tasks and goals.

Play
The emergence of our "playful child" in certain "safe" environments.

Role
The assumption of position relative to each other (e.g., presidnet, janitor, salesman), which permits institutions to function.

Essence
Who we are; not what our role is.

Responsibility/Achievement
The manipulation of things and people to get things going.

Sabbath Time
The acceptance and enjoyment of things and people just as they are.

Law
The provision of "oughts" and "shoulds," which moves communal life from chaos to structure, form, and predicta-. bility. We feel pinched and punished by the "oughts" and "shoulds." The law always convicts us of missing the mark.

Grace
The free gift of redemption, in which we discover that we are accepted just the way we are—we are loved, we are free.

All of these modes reflect either intradependence or extradependence:

Intradependence	*Extradependence*
A state that enables me to move out into the world as a self-sufficient, self-contained human being with all I need to make effective decisions or to bear the burdens of the world. The source of strength on which I depend is inside me ("intra").	A state in which I am dependent upon a source outside of me ("extra") that is caring and trustworthy and allows me to let go, be de-roled, play, and move into Sabbath Time–and an experience of Grace.

The theory states that all of us need to oscillate between these two states. When we fail to oscillate, we get stuck on one side, lose perspective on reality, and go crazy. From time to time, we need to move into a state of extradependence to gain distance from and perspective on our intradependent world, and to see the madness and folly of our lives in that state. We can see that we are taking ourselves, our roles, and our responsibilities too seriously, that there is more to life than just work, roles, and achievement. With this new perspective, we can oscillate back into the world with renewed energy and vision.

Picture a mother and a small child on a park bench. The child clings to the mother and is nurtured by her. After a time, the child lets go and wanders away from the mother to explore and discover new things. Soon the child uses up its store of courage, comes back to the mother to be held and stroked, and, when comforted, wanders off again.

The Grubb Theory states that such an oscillation process is a function not only of childhood but of all ages. All of us need to oscillate like the child between states of intradependence and extradependence and to be healed by the process. However, the presence of a parent figure who is trustworthy, strong, and caring is important for the oscillation to extradependence. Now the plot thickens.

The theory states that the function of religion in society is to manage people's regression to extradependence. *Regression* here describes not a negative event, as in psychological terminology, but a positive one. All of us need to move back to extradependence to stay human and healthy. Consider the symbols and gestures of worship:

Bowing of the head
Folding of the hands
Kneeling
Confession
Receiving absolution
Praying
Listening to scripture
Receiving exhortation in a sermon
Receiving sacraments
Receiving blessings and benedictions

All of these describe a state of extradependence. From their world of intradependence people come to worship bruised and mauled, confused and doubting, needing to be nurtured and cared for—even if for just a while. The familiarity and predictability of the worship service, its cadence, rhythm, and ritual provide what they need. Key to the process of extradependence in worship is the religious authority who affirms the people and the process. In a sense, the pastor leading worship is taking charge of an hour of people's lives so that they can move into a state of extradependence and receive perspective, rest, and healing.

This theory can explain why there are times when lay persons leave church on a Sunday morning not feeling as though they worshipped. Rather than singing old, familiar hymns, the pastor had them learn new hymns. To learn a new hymn you must move back to a state of intradependence. Once the hymn is known well, you can lose yourself in the singing and experience extradependence. The same is true when we learn to use a new liturgy or a new prayer book. The theory explains why there is so much anger and resistance when the church wants to force a new hymnal on its congregations. The reaction comes less from our resistance to new hymns than from our longing for extradependence and the old familiar liturgies and hymns that enable us to experience that state.

When the Roman Catholic Church went from the Latin Mass to the vernacular, they lost millions of members. We Protestants couldn't understand those Catholics who stayed away from their churches because they now had a liturgy in their own language. We were unaware of the enormous stability and continuity that the Latin Mass brought them. They could go anywhere in the world and experience the same extradependence.

In many ways, what clergy are doing for lay people on Sunday morning is to say to them, "Hey, folks, come on in here and let me take care of you for an hour. You have been in charge of your lives all week and you need some rest and perspective. Let's start by singing a hymn." Clergy are in charge during that hour, managing the extradependence for parishioners. To move deeply into extradependence, parishioners must have a caring, trusted pastor to lead them. When the pastor is away on vacation, attendance usually drops dramatically. People have difficulty experiencing extradependence when an unknown person is leading the worship. In short, none of us moves to extradependence until we are certain there is reliable strength at the center of the experience.

In this way, clergy are more like army mess sergeants than commanding generals. We as clergy invite people in out of the battle for a short period of time, offer nourishment, and send them back. We may think they are coming to us for instructions on how to fight the war, and we try to give such instruction. But what brings them back Sunday after Sunday is not the directions we give but our willingness to take care of them for an hour. Within that hour they may receive enough nurture and perspective to go back into the fray.

But where do clergy go for extradependence? Whether clergy are conducting worship, offering individual pastoral care, counseling others, or serving as the chief executive officer of the congregation by conducting business on its behalf, they are in a state of intradependence. Being strong for others, offering consolation or leadership is ninety-five percent of their role. Where can clergy go where someone else is in charge and they can get out of role and be cared for?

Some clergy rely on family or spouse for extradependence. Sometimes doing so is legitimate. However the spouses of clergy are all too aware that having taken care of everyone else, the clergy want to come home and be taken care of themselves. If the spouse who has been working hard at the office or caring for children all day, that spouse may be waiting to be relieved of their role and to experience some extradependence themselves. Clergy need to fill the roles of parent and spouse at home. The constant expectation of extradependence at home places parental and spousal roles and relationships in jeopardy.

Some clergy turn to therapy or spiritual direction to have someone take care of them by giving them their full attention, even if only for an hour a month. I have heard of clergy who go shopping to take a break. At least for a little while someone is waiting on them.

The most common opportunity for extradependence that clergy experience is at continuing education events. Although one hopes that what is offered is worth learning, the important ingredient at such events is leadership. Do the leaders allow clergy participants to move in and out of states of extradependence so that they can get the distance, perspective, rest, and healing they need? Most clergy are unaware of their need for extradependence.

Often when I am leading a seminar I am aware of their need for extradependence. They want me to be in charge. They don't want me to break them up into discussion groups, but would rather have me simply lecture to them. This is particularly true at the beginning of such a seminar. I often find it helpful to have clergy reflect on when they are in a state of extradependence and that state is helpful to them, and when they are not. This reflection helps put them in touch with their own needs for extradependency.

Can clergy experience extradependence by attending worship? Most clergy I talk to have a mixed reaction to this question. I believe it reflects a hazard of being an ordained person who leads in worship every Sunday. We become such experts at leading in worship that we lose our ability to enter a state of extradependence when someone else is in charge. We are either saying to ourselves, "Wow, that was neat. I'm going to remember that next time I'm leading worship," or "He's not doing it right. The rubrics say it should be done this way and he did it wrong." That is not worship. We are more the critics than people who allow themselves to be nurtured and healed by the experience. Some clergy say they are best able to reach a state of extradependent worship in a church tradition radically different from their own. At least some mystery and awe are left when experiencing an unfamiliar liturgy.

Healthy Dependence

A quality support group that meets regularly can furnish a place for this needed extradependence, especially when a trusted, competent facilitator is at the center. Participating clergy can simply attend the group meeting and allow themselves to move into extradependence. Someone else is in charge. Someone else begins the meeting with centering or prayer. Someone else structures a framework by which participants can begin speaking about the complexities of their lives, their fears, joys, points of vulnerability, sense of brokenness. It's not that the facilitator does all the work of caring for those who are there. For a support group to work well, participants must actively listen and interact in a caring way. Yet this mutual caring and support is different from being in charge. In a state of extradependence, we simply allow our natural caring to flow forth from us. Someone else is paying attention to what's happening in the group, for example, whether the group is giving someone more than he or she can handle.

Ideally, the group facilitator should be paid. We all know the kind of energy that goes into monitoring the group process and facilitating decision making. Besides, a good support group is worth some money. It quite likely represents the best professional development investment available to clergy , especially when they have a facilitator who meets the three criteria. This is one area in which a congregation can invest in the development of their pastor. Spending continuing education funds for a support group facilitator is quite legitimate. Some of the most profound insights about parish ministry will come from such a group.

Paid group facilitators is one recommendation the Carlisle Project committee did not accept. Members of the planning committee felt that enough qualified people in the presbytery would offer their services free of charge to facilitate these groups. So far, they have been right. On entering the third season of these groups, the three groups with clearly designated leaders were committed to continue another year.

Still, I am concerned about the fatigue level of the facilitators and the kind of payoff they are getting for offering these services. It really is a labor of love. I hope these facilitators have other sources of extradependence to fill their needs.

Project Evaluation

The groups formed out of the Carlisle Presbytery retreat were carefully monitored for support and learning. In an eighteen-month period I visited each group twice for two hours. During my visits I encouraged group members to express candidly their sense of the strengths and weaknesses of their support community and the process they had adopted. The project team continued to meet to receive reports on the progress of each group and to make recommendations.

What follows is a brief synopsis of each group and the evaluations of its members. It will give you an idea of the variety of support groups that can form in a middle judicatory.

1. The Spiritual Quest Group

The major focus of this group of seven is to foster a deeper awareness of the Spirit's movement in their lives and provide support for the disciplines of prayer. Meetings begin with each person making a personal statement about what is going on in their life. This personal sharing usually provides content for the prayer time that follows. A substantial amount of the prayer time is spent in silence (five to twenty minutes). The group ends with a few minutes of shared prayer.

Comments by Group Members

"I'm in my second year of ministry. I'm an extravert. When I pray I fall asleep. I need a group to help me in my prayer."

"I needed a support group for spiritual deepening. I wanted to get at the Reformed roots of spirituality. As important as prayer is to me, I can't do it without a support community. We have been able to risk this with each other. It's been an exciting adventure."

"I wanted to experiment with prayer with people going in the same direction as I. I have a deep need to be in touch with people who are opening to God. There are not a lot of people waiting to talk about this. I find a lot of support in the prayer of silence."

"Most of my relationships outside our family are joking relationships, especially with other males. I feel I'm at the initial stages of my spiritual development. I find in this group a combination of trust for personal issues and spiritual development."

"I'm not sure how I got here. I was aware of this lack. Being new to ministry, there are limits to relationships with clergy within my system. It's important to me to know that there are people praying for and with me."

"I perceive in Joy and Rebecca something I've been searching for all my life. I just love this group. I'm a lonely person. I usually take on the burdens of others. Here I feel I can say just what I want."

Norms/Nature of the Group Contract

Norms are those unwritten psychological rules that govern behavior in every group. The pattern of community life in this group appears well established. People get down to some basic issues very quickly and then move to prayer. There seems to be a norm that persons are here to support one another. The group enjoys some social time together outside their regular meeting time. They once met for dinner in someone's home, and this past summer they had a picnic together.

The contract for this group is that individuals will be present at every meeting, barring emergencies. Much of the contract for the group is implicit, however; little time was spent working out an explicit contract. There is no termination date for the group. No formal evaluation sessions are planned. Members assume that Paul and Rebecca will continue in their leadership roles. Possibly one of the mistakes in the project was the assurance that I would be dropping by to see the groups. Groups concluded that therefore they didn't need to build in times of evaluation or periodically renegotiate the group contract.

Conclusions/Concerns

This feels like a strong group. It seems to have high energy and commitment. Members are getting what they want from it and more. The leadership is competent and trusted. Members arrive on time and stay for the duration. They have a format that everyone seems to value highly.

This past summer (1989) the group lost one member who was going back to school in another city. The group debated about adding one or two persons. One person had specifically asked if he could join. After much discussion the group decided that the addition did not feel right. Some thought him to be a disruptive spirit and feared the loss of the group climate that everyone appeared to value so much. This seems like a good decision in that participants did not see their group as one that would extend pastoral care at the expense of getting their own support needs met. This group experience is not supposed to be work—it needs to be extradependence.

2. The Gettysburg/Chambersburg Group

This groups consist of seven members all of whom are ordained
Presbyterian clergy. One is female and married to another member of
the group. The tourism in the area is one thing all their congregations
have in common; their section of Pennsylvania has a lot of historical
tradition. The Gettysburg congregation is where Eisenhower used to
worship when in town. Three of the seven members are also part of an
ecumenical evangelical group in the valley. Members are comfortable
with the type of piety and language they use. Three of the members are
new to their congregations, and the group has assisted them in getting
grounded in a new location and in one case a new presbytery.

Comments by Group Members

"Its nice to have clergy friends who go deeper than just hello and
goodbye."

"Up until this point most of my support came from an ecumenical group.
Last year I was called on the carpet by the presbytery. It went to a
positive resolution, but it made me see how little support I had from my
peers within the presbytery.

"There is lots that can make me feel beleaguered. No one feels all the
pressures the same way as another Presbyterian pastor. When gathering
with colleagues we all seem to start from the same base. In a local
ministerium you don't have the same polity in common. This makes this
group unique for me."

"I feel what is said here is not going to come back and hit me in the head
later on. In this area Presbyterians are in a minority. It's a good connec-
tion to have."

"Why are we meeting? Because we were prompted by the project. We
know deep within ourselves that we need this, but it's hard to get a group
like this going. Bill and I used to meet occasionally and said we should
get together more often, but rarely did. It's a good feeling knowing that
there are others in the presbytery who are praying for me."

"I'm here because I sense rapport with this group. I had a rough time coming into this presbytery. I came from a small parish and some felt I couldn't handle this medium-size parish. I want to do well where I am. I know these people can help me. I have a strong call to ministry. I feel I will be supported here in this ministry."

"I had the need for something that was more than process (Presbyterian order)."

Norms/Nature of the Group Contract

There appear to be conflicting norms about starting and ending times. Several group members said they needed more definite parameters—a definite time to begin and a definite time to end. All members are rarely on time, however, and some need to leave early occasionally.

A norm seems to be developing that members come prepared to share something about their parish, something about their family, and something about their personal well-being. After these have been presented, the format calls for shared prayer. There is no agreement about when the group contract is to be renegotiated. Members do not currently take time to evaluate their level of satisfaction with the support group. The group liked my visits because they provided an opportunity for reflection.

Members are open about their appreciation of Chuck's leadership role in facilitating their process and decision making. They like the gentle way he convenes the group. Most clearly understand that the group wouldn't happen without Chuck's initiative. Chuck feels okay about his role as long as people aren't coming just because he sent out notices. The group claims it wants Chuck to be convener and nothing more. They want some guidance when they start and when it's time to close. Chuck thinks that monitoring the group's life takes something away from his ability to benefit from the sessions. Members have not yet arrived at a point where they feel free to confront Chuck and each other. Several people have been predicating their participation on whether or not there are negative experiences. Everyone is placing the responsibility for difficult issues on Chuck, although I have noticed the beginnings of some confrontation through humor.

Conclusions/Concerns

This is another strong group. This fall they begin meeting for their third year. At the next meeting they will discuss including a pastor who has moved into the area. They have decided to stabilize their place of meeting now that they are well acquainted with one another's churches. The Chambersburg church seems most central.

If I have any concerns, they involve Chuck's inability to receive much from this support group. He is obviously investing more of himself in the group than anyone else. The group, however, continues to affirm his leadership and for the present this seems to be enough for him.

3. The Old Veterans in Larger Churches

This group has been meeting for seven years. Its membership has changed over the years, as has its leadership and format. At one point Jim Tice was exercising leadership as an outside facilitator. At the time Jim was a prison chaplain and therapist. He felt the need to withdraw from the group when he became pastor of the Silver Spring church and chair of the Committee on Ministry.

Currently four clergy meet every other week for one and a half hours. One is a retired synod executive who is serving as an interim pastor in a large parish. The other three are pastors who have several in their congregations. Two have been the mainstay of this group over the years. At times only those two were attending the meetings. Members expressed some confusion about why several other clergy left to meet with other support groups.

Comments by Group Members

"This group saved my skin. Several years ago I was burned-out, experiencing enormous emotional turmoil. I had a nasty staff situation that had me completely buffaloed. The group helped me get on top of these issues and encouraged me to take a sabbatical. It was good having Jim Tice as a facilitator at the time as he brought professional counseling skills to the group."

"I am feeling a lot of pressure now. Our program is growing and we don't know what to do. We don't share it all in this group, but it is nice to know there is a place to talk. I have always looked for peer relations. It's a lonely existence without someone who understands. Other clergy really understand."

"As a synod staff person I have not had pastoral experience for nine years. These guys are pros. They have really helped me get back in the swing of things in the parish."

Norms/Nature of the Group Contract

Participants are expected to discuss both their personal and professional lives. They made it clear, however, that this is a professional group and not a social one. They do not try to involve their wives in the group's ongoing life. The group appears to focus mainly on the day-to-day issues of running a large parish with multiple-staff issues and tough counseling situations.

Over the years this group has confronted its members' behavior. I suspect most of this took place while Jim Tice was facilitating. They seem to have learned the gentle art of supporting one another while being candid with each other.

The group claims to have no leader at present. The agenda of the group emerges spontaneously. No notices are sent out, but they do check by phone before meetings. During the meeting I attended, I did notice that Charlie Idler moved the agenda along so that each of us had an opportunity to contribute.

The implicit contract seems to be that this group will meet forever with no built-in evaluation periods along the way. Even though the group is not working as it used to, they have been so helped by it in the past that members want it to continue.

Conclusions/Concerns

I have some concern about the group once Dave's interim has ended. This group will need the infusion of several other group members. It is unclear whether they will have the will to reach out to assimilate one or two new members.

The group seems to be struggling with the absence of Jim's leadership. They have a format now that is working well for them, but will they be able to work through a transition period? They may be unaware of their cynicism toward the presbytery, or of how they are perceived by other clergy in the area. Yet this is an important group for those who remain. They confer on most significant issues arising in their parishes.

4. Charlie's Young Turks

This group was also facilitated by Jim Tice until a year ago; since then it has been getting direction and leadership from Charlie Best. That transfer of leadership was negotiated at the beginning of this project. Currently, the group meets every other week for lunch at Boscov's Restaurant. The group consists of six younger male clergy plus Charlie. The six are all new to ministry and appear to share the feeling that they are all neophytes to the presbytery. At times their counterdependence shows.

   The group talked of adding a woman, yet resisted making the group any larger. Getting enough airtime is difficult enough with six people in an hour and a half. I encouraged them to work on male awareness issues until they find it more appropriate to include some women.

   Currently one of the young men in the group has been diagnosed as having terminal brain cancer. He has resigned from his parish but continues to meet with the group. This past summer the group was meeting more often to give support to Claude. This has given them some difficulty because Claude is deteriorating rapidly and consumes much of the group's energy. They have not taken time to process what effect his dying is having on them.

Comments by Group Members

"I value the opportunity to come here and blow off steam."

"In my community [small rural town] I have no mainline colleagues, that is, none I'm comfortable with. Here I have a chance to share concerns about my parish and my personal life."

"The group really helps put a face on the presbytery. I really don't know where the guts of other professionals are in this place. Ministry can be a very lonely activity. You don't have the opportunity to deal with much personal stuff. This group is a good sounding board. We do a lot of laughing, which heals my soul."

"At seminary we were placed into collegium groups. I hated it. That was forced intimacy. Here I look forward to meeting with the group. I come a long distance, almost from a different culture. This group gives me perspective."

"I don't know how I made it my first sixteen months without this group."

"Seminary geared me to face things alone. We each did our thing there. At the presbytery we put on three-piece suits. Here I can learn to work with colleagues."

"As a new church developer, I'm hanging out there alone. I find I have a strong herd instinct. I'm wired to need this kind of support."

"I need a variety of opinions on tough issues. I need help in what I don't see. This group gives me perspective.

Norms/Nature of the Group Contract

Group members value as little structure as possible, yet they always count on Charlie to bring them back when they get sidetracked. They do not have any built-in termination or recontracting time, nor do they have a contract to critique their life together from time to time.

The group does most of its confronting through humor, which can cut pretty deep. Bill is noted for his candor, and Charlie counts on him to surface some of the tough issues. For the most part group members want to remain congenial and have a good time while they support one another.

The group definitely relies on the leadership of Charlie Best. His most important function is bringing the group back to issues at hand. The group can easily get sidetracked with its humor and its members' varied interests. The group's acceptance of Charlie as leader seems unanimous. Charlie is concerned about being accepted because he was a member of the group like everyone else when Jim Tice was its facilitator.

Conclusions/Concerns

This is a healthy group. The chemistry seems right. Members enjoy each other's company. There is lots of respect for Charlie in his role as facilitator.

Group members may face a crisis when they need to decide on adding members, and that time may come soon. Right now they aren't even talking about it as long as Claude is alive and meeting with them. A death and resurrection time occurs in groups like this when there is a turnover in membership. The addition of one new face can change the whole chemistry of the group. I believe groups without leaders are much more vulnerable to the comings and goings of members than groups with a facilitator.

5. The Inner City Group

At the retreat Fred Widman, chaplain at a local prison, offered to pull together a cadre of clergy serving in the inner city of Harrisburg. Five clergy met and decided to meet every two weeks on Tuesday mornings from nine to ten-thirty in the lounge of a large Presbyterian church.

The first time I met with this group they appeared to be floundering. Only three of the five were present that particular morning. One was not expected. They were having difficulty deciding on a time when they all would be free to meet.

Norms/Nature of the Group Contract

Fred took the initiative to call the group together, but saw no need for leadership beyond this point. He defined the group as the opposite of compulsive. Whoever has something to present is free to do so. Some days when someone brings up an intellectual topic, the group just goes with it. Fred does not see his role as facilitator as including checking whether the group wants to be spending its time this way.

The group appears to be struggling because of a leadership vacuum. Apparently one member, who was absent, had commented that he needed a bit more structure in the meetings. He was working on a Doctor of Ministry degree and was having a time crunch. The two members present at my initial visit commented that it was nice when someone served as timekeeper. One said he would value a stronger leadership role in the group. The lack of strength at the center of the group was having its impact on the trust level.

There is no formal agreement about the length of time the group is to meet or about periodic evaluation times. Members appear to have difficulty expressing what they want from the group.

Conclusions/Concerns

When I met with the group during the next six-month cycle, they seemed to have pulled it together. Five of the participants had found a common link, namely serving congregations of about the same size, three of them in the inner city. One of the pastors had been released from his congregation and was finding support through the group. He continued to meet with the group until it broke up this spring.

When I checked with Fred about the group's start-up again this fall, he had not yet convened the group. He claimed he would see them all at the presbytery meeting at the end of September. He assumed they would want to continue to meet, but he thought they would be down to four participants because the pastor who had been released from his congregation was having difficulty finding work.

The meeting time is still a concern. Fred wanted the group to meet over the lunch hour or in the evenings because he was having more difficulty getting time away from his work at the prison. The group is vulnerable on the issue of agreeing on a meeting time suitable for all.

Fred continues to be good for the group because he is open about his own personal issues and vulnerability. He still convenes the group, although he is laid-back in that responsibility. I believe that the group would grow healthier if Fred would offer more direction to the sharing and decision making.

In spite of my misgivings, this group obviously meets a need for the clergy who are participating. The candor level in the group remains high, which is a good indication of an increasing level of trust. I will feel better about the group when it gets off and running this fall.

6. The Young Couples Group

Once a month on a Friday night, four Presbyterian couples (mainly young clergy with small children) in the western section of the presbytery gather for dinner and conversation. The women in the group do most of the work of preparing the food, cleaning up, and arranging for the next meeting. Besides eating together, the group does not have any formal meeting time. Most of the significant conversations take place in smaller configurations while children run in and out having a great time. The adults and the children do eat separately so dinner conversation often focuses on deeper issues that concern individual members. A major reason for their coming together is the social and intellectual isolation they experience serving churches in rural Pennsylvania.

Comments by Group Members

"This group is fun. At my church we don't have much fun. Eating together is part of the fun."

"In the group, when you mention the "General Assembly," people know what you are talking about. This is not true of our congregations."

"I don't have to be guarded here. Every day at my church I have to be careful what I say."

"For us clergy wives, it's nice to be in a safe haven occasionally."

"It's a great time for our kids."

"It is difficult for me to express myself intellectually in my parish. My people average at the third-grade level."

Norms/Nature of the Group Contract

Everyone comes late. When the group is waiting for the meal to begin, the men usually gather in one room and talk shop while the women gather in the kitchen. Besides grace at the meal, the group prayed together only one other time, when everyone seemed to be going through a crisis. The group breaks up between eight-thirty and nine because of the children.

Most would agree that the Bests and the Griffiths are the backbone of the group. Within this foursome, Eileen Best is seen as the spirit behind the group.

There appears to be no explicit contract about the tenure of the group or times of evaluation.

Conclusions/Concerns

Groups such as this appear to spring up on their own and stay alive as long as they fulfill a need. The obvious problem here is the social and intellectual isolation felt by these young couples, most of whom are serving their first congregation in a rural setting. Groups like this disappear quickly. When I checked on this group, it had been nonexistent for the last six months. The two couples who were giving it leadership left the area at about the same time. The couples that remained seemed to have neither energy nor vision for setting up a new group.

From the outset, the purpose and function of the group was not well articulated. Those who provided leadership saw their main task as getting people together and organizing a meal. Everything else was to happen spontaneously. With a lack of intentionality during meeting time, it is generally difficult to develop enough trust to discuss significant personal or professional issues. If the group had stabilized early, it might have developed this intentionality, however, the group kept changing from meeting to meeting, as members kept inviting any Presbyterian clergy couple in the area who wanted to come. Without group stability, it is hard to develop trust, which is essential for people to be willing to share pain and vulnerability.

Lack of adequate vision at the outset of a group has another drawback, namely that healthy norms and rituals are less likely to emerge. Often a group can still function well even when there is a turnover of leadership because the norms and rituals continue to carry the group process into healthy sharing and support. In this group there were never those norms and rituals that encouraged the sharing of significant material from the lives of individuals.

Conclusions and Learnings of the Carlisle Study

1. Starting Right, Staying Strong

Long after we started the groups we learned that the way we began them was as much a part of their success as anything else. It seems to have been very important that we began these groups with a two-day retreat with as many of the presbytery's clergy present as possible. It helped to have a keynote speaker of national reputation to attract clergy to the event. During the retreat we outlined the theory behind the project and helped participants get in touch with the lack of support in their lives. It seemed helpful to link this presentation with surveys on stress and burn-out and to suggest that support groups were one concrete self-care strategy that clergy could implement in their lives immediately. Pointing out the many benefits of support was also a plus. We explained the many reasons why clergy support groups don't work and together constructed plans to avoid these pitfalls. Before leaving, people made some tentative plans for linking up with others they'd like to have in their support group. This process started four new groups in the presbytery, and each of them is still going strong as they begin their third year.

When the project team met this spring we made plans to form new groups to include clergy who have moved into the area or who have expressed interest in being part of a group but were left out of the first formulation. After several attempts, the team is finding it difficult to get people to commit themselves to testing a group. We seem unable to communicate effectively the importance of a support group or the theory behind those that work well. These clergy may feel a greater risk because they are not as free to choose a support group as were people at the retreat. In one case the committee thought that there were three clergy-women who might form the nucleus of a new group. All three were approached, but not one would assume responsibility for pulling a group together. The committee also believed there was a cadre of like-minded clergy in another part of the presbytery who might form a new group, but the logical person to convene the group kept delaying getting the group together. We seem unable to find ways to motivate these people even to meet to explore possibilities.

The clear disadvantage in forming new groups now is our inability to lay out the pros and cons of peer support groups to the remaining clergy while leaving them the freedom to be with colleagues of their choosing. We are learning how resistant people can be to the suggestion that they join with specific persons to form a group.

The one new group that may have a chance at succeeding is being facilitated by Ken Moe, the pastor elected by the presbytery this spring to fill the newly formed staff position in pastoral care. Clergy seem to find it easier to respond when someone they know and trust takes the initiative to call them together and volunteers to facilitate the meeting. Here again, we can see the extradependence principle at work.

The coordinating committee now appears to be more open to using paid facilitators to start new groups. Jim Tice is thinking about using a facilitator I suggested to organize an ecumenical group for his own benefit. I have suggested an honorarium of $100 per two-hour meeting. With five people in a group meeting twice a month for six months, that amounts to $240 per person, which is a small fee for the kind of perspective and personal support a quality peer group can offer.

2. Non-political Support for Each Group

The groups appeared to value the ongoing attention they received, however periodic, from the project committee and from me as the outside facilitator. It seemed important that somebody cared whether their groups were functioning well. None of the groups were taking the time to evaluate their process formally (a recommendation we should have made at the retreat). Evaluation would usually occur when I visited each group. The questions I asked about such things as leadership, conflict, confrontation, and group process appeared to help them focus and make necessary corrections in their group life. Through those visits and evaluations some of the members came to prize more highly the positive qualities of their groups.

I believe that unless groups and facilitators receive ongoing attention, however minimal, they may flounder, and some will cease to exist. Group facilitators must know who they can call when they are confused about something in their group or when their group feels it is deteriorating. Finding someone to whom a facilitator can turn is difficult, for such support probably cannot come from an official agency of the presbytery. As we learned some time ago, legislated groups generally do not work. The support role can perhaps be filled by Ken Moe in his new position as director of pastoral care in the presbytery. Unfortunately, many middle judicatories do not have a non-political person in that role. I conclude that without consistent effort in this task (namely supporting existing clergy groups and, in whatever ways work, helping to initiate new groups and connect them with a competent facilitator), many worthwhile groups will flounder and disband and clergy morale will drop accordingly. Possibly a knowledgeable person outside the judicatory can fulfill this role.

3. Better Contracting Up Front

The project could have been more helpful to existing groups by encouraging more explicit contracting as groups began. In retrospect, we could have provided a more explicit model with elements that make for healthy groups. We could have recommended that as each group began it take time to become clear about

—The role of the facilitator if they have one, or the leadership role if they don't. If no one is designated as leader, the group should reach some agreement about necessary leadership functions and who will perform them.

—How long they are willing to experiment to see if the group is going to work. Beyond this there should be regular times when they will review their level of satisfaction and either disband or recontract.

—How they will go about critiquing their ongoing life to ensure it is meeting their needs.

There are ways to overdo contracting as well. Before a group really gets under way and nurtures people, members may be scared off because someone is trying to nail down all contingencies. People are not sure they want to commit themselves before they know whether or not the group is for them. Beyond agreeing about the three issues listed above and some basic decisions about time, place, and frequency of meeting, I would recommend working things out as the group life develops. What's important is an agreement for frequent evaluations so that the group is continually fine-tuning its corporate life to make it more fulfilling for all.

This project has taught me a lot about the importance of healthy norms and rituals in clergy support groups. We human beings seem to crave a ritualized life. We like patterns so that we can anticipate the flow of events. Rituals keep families together and provide meaning. Rituals in our congregations bind us together more than doctrine or belief statements. How the group gathers, how individuals greet one another, how the group addresses the meaningful things of our lives, how the meetings begin to wind up, and how members depart—all of these elements develop into either healthy, life-supporting rituals or patterns that are not nurturing and satisfying.

I believe that the group of veteran clergy in large congregations developed some healthy norms and rituals when Jim Tice took them through some tough places. Now, even though Jim has withdrawn as a leader, that group continues to function well, and they are beginning again this fall with great determination to continue their healthy patterns. I also believe that the clergy couples' group folded because it did not develop norms and rituals that were worth preserving once its key leadership left.

Norms are most difficult to talk about because those of us who are the most immersed in a group's life are the least conscious of them. If you have ever worked as an outside consultant to a congregation, you know how hard it is to bring to the congregation's awareness the norms by which members conduct themselves. Yet you also know that to raise the quality of life within any congregation, you must work directly on those norms. The quality of any support community depends on the norms at work within that group. Periodic evaluations are probably the best way for a group to get at its norms and see if they are leading members to greater health. It is also helpful to periodically invite an outsider in to assist the group in reflecting on its norms.

Starting right is to begin a support group with clear intentionality about the kind of norm, or unwritten rule, we want as a group working together.

Staying strong requires building in critique points frequently to consistently upgrade the quality of the norms.

4. Leadership Strength at the Center

This project has convinced me more than ever that the key to beginning effective clergy support groups is leadership. I believe this is especially true for clergy groups because most clergy find themselves depleted by continually being in an intradependent state, always giving to others with little time to replenish themselves. Clergy need a group in which they are free not to be in role or in charge.

After two years the groups with effective facilitators appear to be the strongest. Those with less effective facilitators appear to be floundering. In some cases we failed in the project to clearly outline to facilitators what kind of leadership is most likely to produce a good effect in their group. We are learning.

5. The Model Can Be Replicated

At the conclusion of this project I find myself eager to replicate it in another judicatory—at a fraction of the cost. The Carlisle Project cost $22,483. I am convinced that the morale in Carlisle Presbytery is higher than it was before because twenty-two more clergy in that presbytery now have ongoing support groups. The quality of those twenty-two congregations will be enhanced because their clergy are enriched in this way.

Middle judicatory executives are probably highly aware of how many clergy are trying to do ministry without much support. Many executives are baffled about why those clergy don't get themselves into a support group. Their recommendations that clergy in certain sections of the judicatory get together and become a support system for one another often fall on deaf ears. I believe it is ludicrous to think you can simply herd clergy together and have them be a support group for one another just because they happen to serve at nearby churches. However, I now feel we have a model for encouraging effective support groups within a given judicatory.

I would be intrigued by an ecumenical approach to this problem. I could envision working with four or five middle judicatory executives in a metropolitan area to structure ecumenical groups using this model. Competent outside facilitators would need to be identified in the area. An initial clergy retreat would need to be planned—one that would have the greatest possibility of attracting as many clergy in those systems as possible. Once we outlined the theory and rationale, the clergy could begin clustering with like-minded folk. It would be worth driving across the city to be with other clergy with whom you feel comfortable. I still believe it is the best of all worlds if the group facilitator is paid; if so it might cost those clergy something to be in such a group. The middle judicatories could decide if they wanted to invest in the formation of these group and possibly subsidize them. Some groups (for instance, those made up of clergy from poorer congregations) might need more support than others.

I not only believe groups are workable, I also believe there is a good supply of clergy group facilitators out there, many working in non-parish settings, who would love to contribute their skills to the church in this way. Many of them would be willing to work for much less than their normal fee in such an effort.

The Carlisle Project has provided insights that will serve the broader church. Through the project, I was especially encouraged to find people who not only can empathize with the pain and fatigue of clergy, but who then become committed to doing something concrete about it. That kind of effort and energy benefits us all, for we are all one body.

Before I present suggestions for your forming support groups, I would like to discuss a key issue in assembling potential group members. Although the Carlisle Project did not take this issue into account when forming groups, it is, nevertheless, worth considering. The issue is the relationship between personality and support in a group.

NOTES

1. Robert N. Bellah, Richard Madsen, William M. Sullivan, Ann Swidler, and Steven M. Tipton, *Habits of the Heart* (New York: Harper & Row, 1986).
2. M. Scott Peck, *A Different Drum* (New York: Simon & Schuster, 1987).

CHAPTER IV

Type and Support

by Roy M. Oswald based on input from Otto Kroeger

It's always fun working with Otto Kroeger. He is genuinely funny , yet as smart as can be, and I always learn something new from our time together. We share twenty-six years of history as colleagues beginning when we were ordained clergy in the Lutheran Church in America. The war stories we swap dating back to the time when we were pioneering human relationships training in the church have even us wondering if they are apocryphal.

Otto and I co-authored the book *Personality Type and Religious Leadership,* published by The Alban Institute. This chapter could be seen as an addendum to that book. We are pleased that church leaders are finding the book helpful.

From my perspective, Otto is one of the most knowledgeable people in the country now on the subject of the Myers-Briggs Type Indicator (MBTI). *Type Talk,* which he coauthored with his wife and partner Janet Thuesen, has just come out in paperback after a good year in hardback. It is so well received that he and Janet are currently under contract to produce a second book, *Type in the Work Place.*[1]

Otto and I spent an afternoon talking about type and support. We wanted to explore the strengths and liabilities each MBTI type brought to the issue of support. We were also interested in the kinds of support the various types would need most. Finally, we wanted to see if we could identify the kinds of resistance to being part of a support community and to asking for help that would arise from the eight type preferences. For those of you who are unfamiliar with the MBTI, I will explain the type preferences as we go along.

Extraverts and Introverts

Extraverts prefer to focus on the outer world of people and things; they get their energy from interaction with the outer world. Their battery runs down when they have to spend too much time by themselves—contemplating, thinking, writing, preparing. They can only take so much solitude before they call a friend or wander into a place in the house or office where there are other people.

Introverts, however, prefer to focus on the inner world of thoughts, feelings, and impressions. Introverts get their energy from being alone and escaping to their inner world. Introverts can be very skillful at social relationships and can even be the life of a party, yet all the time they are expending energy in the outer world their battery is running down. To maintain their balance they need chunks of time by themselves so they can manage all that they want or need to do in the outer world.

It shouldn't surprise us that Introverts and Extraverts have different support needs and therefore will function quite differently within a support group. Among parish clergy, there is a disproportionately high number of Introverts. Even though tests of the general population indicate that approximately seventy-five percent are Extraverts and twenty-five percent are Introverts, among clergy we usually find that close to forty-five percent are Introverts and fifty-five percent are Extraverts. Some find this surprising because the parish ministry is clearly more suited to Extraverts. This is not to say that Introverts do not make effective clergy. On the contrary, we have many excellent clergy who are Introverts. Yet a heavy toll is exacted of Introverts by the constant need to be engaged with people in such a wide variety of settings. Thus, clergy who are Introverts burn out much more quickly than clergy who are Extraverts. Accordingly, a solid support group can be invaluable to Introverts–first, because without it they may be unaware that they are moving toward burnout, and second, once burned-out, they can receive support from the group that enables them to do those self-care things needed to get out of that hole.

The problem, however, is that Introverts will not seek support nearly as quickly as Extraverts. Perhaps Introverts don't need as much support as Extraverts when things are going well. When a critical incident occurs in the parish, Extraverts will to want to go somewhere to talk about it. In talking it out, the Extraverts often find out what they really think about that incident. Introverts, on the other hand, will usually want to be alone so they can figure out what they think and feel about the event. After they have thought it through, they may or may not decide to talk it over with someone else. If they believe they have arrived at the right conclusion, they will have much less need to talk about the incident than clergy who are Extraverts.

This is where the support needs of these two types may differ greatly. Because Introverts do not perceive the need for a lot of support on the surface, they tend not to do the hard work of finding appropriate support persons or groups for use when times of crisis arise. Extraverts, on the other hand, tend to dump their problems on whoever is around, whether they are ready to listen or not. But while, Extraverts tend to receive a lot of support on an informal basis, they also do not do the hard work of establishing intentional support communities. Of the two, however, Extraverts are much more likely to respond to the suggestion of a potential support group. Parish clergy have so little time to themselves, especially when they are married and have children, that clergy Introverts think long and hard before they are willing to commit to regular meetings with another group.

Once in an intentional support group, Extraverts are bound to take up more of the air time than Introverts. With Extraverts, "What you see is what you get." They are an open book, ready to let it all hang out and therefore far less likely to struggle to decide what is appropriate to share in this group and what is not. Because they do tend to dominate and are willing to reveal more of themselves, they will probably gain more from an intentional group than Introverts.

Introverts will struggle about what is appropriate to tell the group and what is not. They are much slower to ask for help and often carry an ongoing concern about not burdening their friends with unimportant matters. They tend to categorize many of the things that worry them as unimportant in the eyes of others. Thus, Introverts will benefit much more from a structure that facilitates a sharing process or by having a facilitator who ensures that people stay with the topic and the agreed-upon time each member is allotted.

Extraverts are at home with a free-flowing "jump in when you feel like it" group. Even when the talk is rapid and engaging, Extraverts will get their agenda on the table. Introverts are less likely to do so; they easily become involved in other people's issues and concerns, leaving their own unexpressed. Introverts are always disadvantaged in a free-flowing discussion with Extraverts because they want to think it through before expressing an opinion, and by the time they have formulated their opinion, the group agenda has shifted. Extraverts want to talk things through rather than think them through. What the Introverts do inside, the Extraverts do outside. Thus, Extraverts are much more likely to jump into a discussion with only half-formulated ideas, ready to talk things out to find out what they really believe or think.

As in leaving a party, Introverts and Extraverts will probably leave the group time with different regrets. Extraverts will regret having said too much, possibly having opened mouth only to exchange feet. Only in retrospect will they realize that someone else's feelings got stomped on in the process. Introverts will regret not having captured the moment and said something important. Possibly they had something helpful or encouraging to say to another, yet found the meeting ended with it still unexpressed. Or possibly they came ready to reveal a vulnerable part of their life but kept waiting for the right opportunity to share it, which never arrived. Thus they leave with the burden still completely on their shoulders, with no help or support from others.

This is where a facilitator can make all the difference in the world for the Introverts. The skilled facilitator can set the stage by asking everyone to take ten minutes to express the burdens and joys of their lives since the last meeting. When Introverts expect this structure from a facilitator, they will have put a lot of thought into what they want to reveal to the group that day. More than likely, it will be deeply personal, and it will be expressed in an economy of words. Extraverts generally receive much when Introverts are given the format through which they can share their rich inner world with group members.

Introverts and Extraverts can become quite perturbed with one another when they try to function within the same support group. Introverts can become sarcastic about all the verbiage from Extraverts. Because much of their speech is exploratory, Extraverts don't mean much of what they say in the first place. One of the attractions of being part of a support group is the opportunity to air things so members can become clear about what they really can affirm. Introverts, on the other hand, rarely say anything until it is thought through and worded just right. They can easily become annoyed when old "motor mouth" takes the group on another merry-go-round, including repeating what he or she has said three or four times. Introverts can also become upset when they try to express themselves, but keep getting cut off, or when the group is not sensitive enough to notice the nonverbal signs that indicate they have something important to say. It can be tiring for an Introvert trying to move against the nonstop tide of Extravert garbage. When the Introverts see that the Extraverts aren't even listening to each other, Introverts may lose hope that Extraverts would listen to them.

Extraverts, on the other hand, can get fed up with Introverts who seem to be just sitting there and never really entering in. Extraverts may soon feel overexposed and vulnerable because they have been expressing their feelings readily while the Introverts have said practically nothing. Extraverts can also get tired of stopping to encourage the Introverts to climb aboard. The Extraverts can't understand why the Introverts don't jump on like everyone else. Extraverts may also feel hurt when no one senses how badly they are hurting when they reveal their feelings. Although the Extraverts may have been merely engaging in "bitch and brag," underneath they expected someone to notice that they were in pain and draw them out on the subject. Here a skilled facilitator can be a great resource to Extraverts.

Every support group should be fortunate enough to have a good mixture of Introverts and Extraverts. Extraverts will feel "listened to" by the Introverts. Introverts will provide a question here or a comment there to keep the Extraverts on track. In the end, the Extraverts will feel much more confident about facing the issue waiting for them back in the real world.

Extraverts will help the Introverts recognize their own needs and the importance of expressing and exploring them. Once the personal experiences of the Introverts are out on the table, the spontaneous reactions of the Extraverts to them will generally give the Introverts a few new ways to view the issues. Introverts will learn that they cannot always figure things out by themselves. Once again, a competent, sensitive, and safe facilitator can bring out the best in both types so that the gifts of each can be more fully appreciated.

Sensors and INtuitives

Sensors like to focus on the present reality and on the information brought to them by their senses. They are realists who want to be grounded in the tangible aspects of the world around them.

INtuitives would prefer to focus on possibilities and relationships. They are less interested in what is actually before them than in the meaning it suggests.

In the general population, Sensors outnumber iNtuitives by three to one, however, in the ordained ministry iNtuitives far outnumber Sensors. (This is less true in more fundamentalist, conservative denominations.) According to our latest statistics at The Alban Institute, out of 1,500 clergy tested, 69 percent were INtuitives and 31 percent were Sensors.

Sensors and iNtuitives approach the support issue with differing needs. Of the Sensors in the ordained ministry, 90 percent will be SJs (Sensing/Judging types). We have so few SP (Sensing/Perceiving) clergy that we will focus on those who are SJs. SJs are the perfect example of role clarity. "A place for all and all in their place," is a perfect SJ way of viewing parish ministry. With this attitude, it is difficult to own any personal needs. Why would such clergy need support when they bring this kind of clarity to their work? SJs are more likely to go the route of the martyr than to admit they have any needs and ask their colleagues for help.

For Sensors to join a colleague group and feel that it is worth their while, they will need to leave each group meeting feeling they have received something tangible and practical that is going to help them in their ministry that week. They will believe the group meeting was useful because they learned one or two concrete ways they might approach something they have been struggling with. In short, the group didn't just theorize about support—they got right down to supporting.

INtuitives, whether NFs (iNtuitive/Feelers) or NTs (iNtuitive/Thinkers), are great at theorizing about support and their needs for it, but are always too busy to be involved. With iNtuitives, there is always one more thing to do, one more possibility to chase down. This will especially be true for NTPs (iNtuitive/Thinker/Perceivers) and NFPs (iNtuitive/Feeler/Perceivers), who will usually get waylaid by other things rather than admit their need for a support group and make some concrete moves to establish one.

Sensors and iNtuitives, if in the same group, will view support from two different perspectives. INtuitives in the group, after working with a group member and offering every possible perspective from which to view the present issue, will say, "Boy, wasn't that a great meeting!" Sensors may say, "Baloney! We didn't even give John a hug before he left this morning. In addition, we didn't offer him one concrete way he can approach the issue on Monday." It's not that the NTs or the NFs would be against giving John a hug, but they will want to think abstractly about the issue again later.

We can see the Sensor Saint Paul in I Corinthians 13 taking on the iNtuitive about what constitutes real help. "If I speak with the tongues of men and of angels, [the high verbal skills of the iNtuitive] but have not love, I am nothing." Love is concrete action or else it is a "noisy gong or a clanging symbol." For iNtuitives, especially NFs, love is a feeling. For Sensors, love is doing. Sensors and iNtuitives may need to face this dilemma if they are in the same peer support group. A group facilitator who is familiar with MBTI theory can help a group capitalize on the strengths of each type while limiting potential sources of tension.

When things are working well in a peer group and the trust is high, Sensors will be able to help iNtuitives face difficulties with realism. They will help iNtuitives keep track of essential details and notice what needs immediate attention. Sensors will remind iNtuitives to read the fine print in a contract or to come to terms with the bottom line on each issue. Also, Sensors will usually bring up pertinent facts that may be passed over too lightly by the iNtuitive.

INtuitives can help Sensors look at new possibilities in every situation. With every problem raised by a Sensor, the iNtuitives will supply loads of ingenuity and possible innovative solutions. INtuitives can also help Sensors read the signs of coming change and be more prepared for the future. INtuitives will encourage Sensors to bring some enthusiasm and zest to their difficulties and help them see that the joys of the future are worth looking forward to.

Thinkers and Feelers

Thinkers like to arrive at their conclusions through logic and objective analysis. What's logical in one area of life will need to be congruent with their analytical conclusions in other areas of life. They prize distance and objectivity in important decisions.

Feelers like to base their judgments on personal values. They prize what's important to them more highly than logic. Feelers are more likely than Thinkers to ask, Who is going to be affected by this decision? Based on the answer, Feelers may alter the decision they were going to make. Feelers tend to be more person-oriented.

Thinkers tend to be more independent and therefore will have less need to belong to a peer group. Should they perceive a personal need for such a small supportive community, it will usually be to help them work through their thinking on problematic issues. Thinkers carry the belief that if their head is on straight, they can handle all issues. They may be out of touch with how badly they are hurting about an issue or the relational landmines that await the priorities they have set for themselves. They may also miss the effect their decisions will have on specific people. Feelers could be of great assistance to them in all of these instances.

Feelers, on the other hand, are great at offering support to others but poor at asking for or even receiving it themselves. If they are Extravert/Feelers, the idea of getting together with a group of chosen colleagues will hold lots of appeal, but the appeal will be for experiencing fellowship rather than having a place to ask for and receive help. "Let's just talk idly about this a bit rather than getting into my specific issues," they might say to themselves in effect.

When Feelers bring problems to a peer support group, nine out of ten will be relational issues. The lives of Feelers are consumed by efforts to get all the relationships in their lives working well. They may be out of touch with the fact that their theoretical base for approaching parish problems is off or that their implicit theology (what they are doing) is not congruent with their explicit theology (what they are saying). Feelers may also be so overwhelmed by the sheer volume of emotional issues facing them in the parish that they have lost any objectivity in the situation. Thinkers could be of great assistance to them in all of these instances.

In the best of all worlds, when there is a good mixture of Thinkers and Feelers in a peer support group, Thinkers can be of enormous help to Feelers in accepting that someone on their staff needs to be fired. Usually this staff situation is a nightmare for Feelers, and Thinkers can help bring some objectivity and logic to the task. Thinkers can also be like a rock to Feelers in helping them stand firm against opposition. Feelers, on the other hand, can be of great help to Thinkers in working through relationships to deeper reconciliation. Feelers can help Thinkers forecast how others will feel when certain things are said or done. Parish ministry sometimes rises or falls on how well people relate. Feelers can help Thinkers work through some of the complexities of dysfunctional relationships.

In short, Thinkers in the group can help Feelers get their heads straight. They can help Feelers get out of the morass of their feelings for a moment to see clearly a few logical consequences of their behavior. The Feelers in the group can help the Thinkers get their hearts straight. Thinkers may be hurting and not know it. It may take a Feeler simply saying, "Gosh, Bill you really must be suffering about your family right now." Helping the Thinkers shed a tear or two about their pain can be a real ministry.

Judgers and Perceivers

Judgers like a planned and organized approach to life. They tend to want things settled and decided. Perceiving types like an adaptable, flexible, and spontaneous approach to life. They like to stay open to new experiences.

Judgers and Perceivers may agitate each other in trying to get a peer support group going. The Judgers will want to get everything organized, right down to the last minute. The Perceivers will resist that, finding it too confining. Perceivers will probably insist that it's in the spontaneous movement of the group that important issues will arise.

A key conflict related to structure and process may need to be averted when the group is formed. Perceivers will want to experience the group doing something together before deciding about commitment to the group or the group agenda and priorities. Perceivers always feel they don't have enough information to arrive at a conclusion. The information they will want in the beginning comes from experiencing the group in action. If the group feels right to them, they may be willing to commit to meeting regularly.

It is difficult for Judgers to enter a new experience without knowing what's ahead. Entering into a group cold turkey without a plan, a contract, or an understanding may seem like madness to them, like being in a nudist colony for the first time without knowing any of the protocol. They will want a few things nailed down before they are willing to give it a try.

This is where a skilled facilitator can offer a compromise to Judgers and Perceivers. The facilitator can lay out a provisional structure for the first few sessions, meeting the Judgers' needs, yet can say that the group will be reflecting on this structure at each session to see if the process fits expectations. Telling the group that no one needs to commit to the whole six-month contract until after the group has met for several times is going to make the Perceivers breathe a whole lot easier.

Once the group is off the ground, Judgers and Perceivers can offer each other a healthy balance. Perceivers can help Judgers see that they don't need to be in control at all times, in fact, some of the more important things in life can happen when they relinquish control. Perceivers can also help Judgers ride a little more easily with ambiguity and uncertainty. They may help Judgers see the advantages of allowing things to remain unsettled and undecided for slightly longer periods of time.

Judgers, on the other hand, can help Perceivers see the advantages of having a plan. They can also help them see the enjoyment of parish ministry even when they are not on the cutting edge of something new. There is grace and beauty in the old and the familiar. Judgers may help Perceivers get in touch with their constant restlessness and anxiety about commitment. In both marriage and ministry, Judgers can help Perceivers stay out of trouble by helping them think through the long-term consequences of following through with their spontaneous notions.

Both Judgers and Perceivers can experience burnout for different reasons, and they can help each other to get out of that debilitating malady. Judgers can become overcommitted and feel trapped by trying to fulfill all the commitments they made. Judgers can bring rigidity to their sense of obligation. Even though they know they need some rest or time off, they have a hard time living with themselves if they don't follow through on what they consider to be their responsibility.

Perceivers can help Judgers see the variety of options they have for cutting back to a more reasonable load.

Perceivers can also become overextended, but they get there in a different way. Because they value trying new things so highly, they end up starting much more than they can manage. Perceivers value their freedom highly because when they are free they can explore all the options that interest them. In no time, however, all these new projects start demanding more time and attention. Suddenly, Perceivers feel suffocated by all the demands, and they can become depressed quite quickly without relief from them. Judgers can be a real resource to Perceivers in helping them organize their parishes in such a way that the follow-through on these new ventures is taken up by volunteers and other structures. Perceivers generally can use all the organizational help they can get, and organizing is the forte of Judgers.

The Healthy Mixture

From one perspective, the best peer support group would represent all eight preferences. Such heterogeneity would make for a rich mix of ideas, processes, and approaches. Yet experience has shown that such groups have difficulty functioning well together over extended periods of time. We may give lip service to variety in perspectives and differing approaches to life, but when we get down to where we are hurting badly, we want to be surrounded by our own type and temperament. It's our own type that will understand us more profoundly and be able to walk in our moccasins.

In many groups the issue may not be difference but sameness. Birds of a feather flock together, as the saying goes, and like types will probably find themselves in the same group. This is especially true if you follow a suggestion in the next chapter of this book, namely that two people who feel they can trust and care for one another meet and decide on two or three others they would feel comfortable including in such a peer group. The probability of these two people choosing persons of like type is fairly high.

From a typological perspective, it would be more helpful over the long haul for there to be some heterogeneity in the group, for all the reasons mentioned above about how opposites can really be of help to one another. Yet pressing for the extremes in heterogeneity is not going to work because of the constant, hard work that will be needed to keep the trust level high in such a group. (The data indicate that people with the exact opposite four-letter types may initially be attracted to one another but that their marriages tend to have more casualties than those of people who marry more similar types).

If you have an introductory knowledge of the MBTI, Otto and I suggest trying to press for some variety in the group. Having two letters in common with another person makes for enough similarity and enough differences so that support and stimulation can be present. We would recommend having at least two of the four temperaments in the same group (SJ, SP, NF, NT). Having a mix of Introverts and Extraverts, plus Judgers and Perceivers, is a good idea. All of this is contingent upon your having some real options in your area among persons with whom you would be willing to reveal pain and vulnerability. From our perspective, trust must have higher priority than heterogeneity.

In the male support community that was most helpful to me for five years, the group consisted of two INFPs, one INFJ, and one ENTJ. We were all iNtuitives, which may have contributed to some fairly spaced-out discussions, yet we loved every minute. The group had one Thinker, who often brought some clear reasoning to our highly theoretical discussions. We had a healthy balance between Judgers and Perceivers, which made for order and openness. We were often struck by how the Judgers came to receive help with a decision, whereas the Perceivers came to have the group open up more options for them. To accommodate the Introverts, we would usually begin the meeting with a chant and five minutes of silence. After that, the agenda flowed freely with few periods in which no one had anything to say.

Being sensitive to the relationship between type and support can help as you begin forming a support group. Having given you some thoughts to ponder about personality types and their role in groups, I will now present some practical steps and suggestions about establishing support.

NOTES

1. If you want a very helpful audiocassette on your MBTI type, you can order it from Otto Kroeger Associates, 3605-C Chain Bridge Road, Fairfax, VA 22030. Phone (703) 591-6284. It is part of their TypeWatching Series. If you wish to be certified to purchase and administer the MBTI, you will need a four-day intensive training program. The training offered by Otto Kroeger Associates is some of the best available.

CHAPTER V

Getting Started

Individual Clergy

If as a parish pastor you are aware of how your ministry could be helped by your membership in a strong, caring, peer fellowship, I would recommend the following. Think about one other clergy person in your area with whom you would be willing to trust your pain and vulnerability. Take time to choose this person carefully. It should be someone whom you respect, yet someone with whom you would feel free to reveal the truth about yourself. Would you be willing to talk about not only parish problems with this person but also such things as your falling in love with a parishioner even though you are already married, a drinking problem you discovered in your family, or your discovery that your kids are on drugs? Even if you have no pressing personal problems now, it can be pretty lonely when they do occur and you discover you are not comfortable revealing them to the group that is supposed to be part of your support network.

When you have identified someone, call the person and ask to have lunch. At the lunch meeting, lay out your need for a reliable support group as well as your vision for what an effective support group could do for you.

Begin to explore whether this clergy person might also be in need of such a support community and some of the objectives for such a group.

It's important at this point to distinguish between forming a support group that focuses on personal and professional issues and one that deals only with professional issues. Some clergy groups, for example, meet regularly for Bible study and sermon preparation. Members may become involved with each other personally as a result of this interaction, but the main focus of the group is honing professional skills. Other groups meet to present case studies of critical incidents in the parish. I am highly supportive of the case study approach for gaining role clarity in a parish setting. Yet the focus of this kind of group is professional development, and personal support may have to happen around the edges of this focus.

A group that intentionally meets to be of personal support to its members can go both ways. Members of such a group have a choice, for example, of either telling the group about some painful aspect of their personal or relational life or talking about a problem they are having in their parish. Whatever seems to be consuming their energy at the moment is appropriate for discussion. The disadvantage of such a group is that it focuses mainly on personal issues, and professional issues tend to be squeezed out. Which do you need more right now, personal support or professional development? The answer to that question will determine the kind of support group you begin to form intentionally. It depends on where life seems to be pinching you the most right now.

At times I have recommended to individual pastors that they ask a group of colleagues to assist them in working through a difficult issue in their lives. Some were clergy who were getting up in years and needed to get a call to another congregation. A myth circulating within denominational systems these days is that if you are over fifty, it's next to impossible to get moved to another parish. I believe that clergy, whatever their age, can find calls to other congregations but that they need some support in facing the number of rejections they will receive until the right church comes along. Clergy generally enter this process halfheartedly, updating their dossier, and then sitting back and waiting. When they cannot even get a church to interview them or when they come in second two or three times, they get so discouraged that they give up, become depressed, and do little to get moved. Yet when they have a group of three or four people meeting regularly with them and asking them what they have done lately to get themselves moved, these clergy usually can persist until a new call comes their way. The pinch in this case is very specific and calls for a special kind of support community over a limited period of time. The nature of the support function also determines who is asked to participate.

A support group focused on helping someone get a call to another parish appears to be strictly professional. But there are many personal issues involved, for example, one's level of self-esteem, one's physical health and appearance, the quality of one's family life. Such issues can play important roles in getting that new call. In the process of searching, the pastor wanting to move may uncover some serious emotional issues that have been lying dormant for years. These may need to be addressed before the pastor becomes attractive to another parish. Thus, my suggestion would be to form a personal support group that deals with professional issues, rather than a professional support group.

The difference is subtle, yet important. The type of group will determine whom you ask to lunch to begin exploring the possibility of such a group, as well as who is asked to participate beyond that person. I know some people I respect immensely as church professionals. I know I could learn from them should we find ourselves in an appropriate learning format. Yet these are not the people to whom I would choose to reveal the inner struggles of my soul. Conversely, the people I might trust to reveal the struggles of my soul to may not be the most competent at helping me face a tough professional issue.

What's most pressing for you right now? Are you having difficulty putting a sermon together each week, or do you need some outside perspective on a rocky marriage? Do you need some coaching to get you through a change effort in your parish, or do you need some help finding out why your ministry seems to have run out of gas? Do you find yourself agonizing over your inability to work with certain parishioners, or is trying to be all things to all people starting to get to you? If in any of these questions you were to choose the first element, then doing some case study work with some clergy colleagues would be more helpful. If you would choose the second element, simply having some clergy colleagues listen to your story and respond spontaneously would be more helpful.

If the person you are having lunch with would also like to form such a group with some specific goals in mind, the next step is to find the right people with whom to launch the effort. Between the two of you, see if you can think of three or four other people with whom you could be open about pain, vulnerability, and confusion. I recommend that the group be no larger than six: when the group meets it is important that each person have quality air time. When you get more than six it can become too cumbersome and time-consuming.

The other people you choose to add to the group are crucial. To misjudge persons at this point is essentially to kill the group's chances of bringing perspective and vitality to its members. One person can foul up a group's ability to trust and therefore diminish members' willingness to share pain and vulnerability. Trust for me is the hallmark of an effective support group. Without trust, which is followed by our willingness to reveal where we are hurting, a group quickly degenerates into a "bitch and brag" group. Perhaps I should not disparage groups that meet for social reasons other than personal support. Having places where one can catch up on the gossip of the denomination or simply find out what others are doing in their churches can also be important. In the long run, however, I believe that what I and other church professionals need are groups trustworthy enough for us not to have to work to hide what is really going on in our lives.

This is no time to decide to be pastoral to a clergy colleague down the road who is hurting. There are other ways to offer pastoral support than by inviting a colleague into your support group. If you conclude that this person would effectively block your group from moving to depth, do not feel constrained to invite this person.

My experience has been that ecumenical groups work better than denominational groups. There seems to be greater competitiveness between clergy within the same denomination. It is also probably easier to find like-minded clergy in your area if you are willing to cross denominational boundaries.

As Otto Kroeger and I suggested in the last chapter, you should consider the mix of personality types when forming a group.

You may also find that you have to get into your car and drive a considerable distance to be with clergy where the match is right. In the long run, it will be more beneficial to drive an hour to be with the right group than to have the wrong group within fifteen minutes of your church. How often the group meets may depend upon distance. The most popular support group rhythm in Carlisle Presbytery is meeting for two hours every two weeks. That seemed to provide enough continuity for those groups while not taking huge chunks of time out of work schedules. The male support group to which I belong meets for four hours once a month (eleven to three with lunch at a local restaurant). The Phrogs group meets twice a year for an overnight because people are driving in from as far as Philadelphia and North Carolina.

Once you and your lunch partner have chosen others to invite to be part of the support group, begin to talk about possible group facilitators. Once again, the choice is crucial. All members of the group need to trust this person's ability to see them through the inevitable road blocks encountered on the way to meaningful community. Begin looking for facilitators among people such as hospital or prison chaplains, pastoral counselors, faculty at local church colleges, former clergy now engaged in secular employment, or retired clergy. I recommend that this person have some experience as a parish pastor. This way the facilitator won't be bringing simplistic solutions to complex role issues. Occasionally a lay person with good human relations skills possesses a comprehensive view of the pastoral role and could serve you well as a support group facilitator. A fee of $100 for each two-hour session is recommended, although some of these professionals may volunteer to do it for much less. I recommend paying them something just to help maintain role clarity. These facilitators may find that their participation in the group may do a great deal for them personally, yet their primary role is to facilitate support of members for each other.

I have met more than one person around the country who told me a group they had belonged to was facilitated by the local hospital chaplain, who did it free. The group of clergy all met in the hospital facility, which was also a plus because it got the clergy out of their parish settings. In certain settings with the right hospital chaplain, this setup is a natural. Chaplains usually have CPE (Clinical Pastoral Education) training and thus have some of the key skills necessary for facilitating such a group. Additionally, the local hospital often has an investment in sustaining good relations with area clergy. Hospital administrators consider this a way in which they can serve the local community. The people who told me about these groups also talked about the quality of the support they felt from such a group, once again demonstrating the principle of clergy needing a group in which they can experience extra-dependence. Many hospital chaplains are naturals at facilitating extra-dependence.

One consideration about using the local hospital chaplain is the amount of control you have over the group's makeup. I think it would still be important to identify those persons with the potential for developing trust and asking the chaplain to facilitate that group, rather than having the chaplain call together the group of clergy that he or she would like to work with. The chaplain may feel uncomfortable with excluding certain clergy in the community from the group.

Having found a facilitator, put together a budget showing how much such an experience might cost each individual over a six-month period. Either of you may be able to obtain some outside funding to reduce the individual cost. Your denominational executive might know of a source of funding. Middle judicatory executives often are aware of the lack of support that exists for certain clergy, yet don't know how to make support available to them. Offering matching funds to pay for a facilitated group is one concrete way they can help.

You should also feel free to use some of your continuing education funds for this experience. You will probably learn more from this group than from any seminar, and this could be a very wise use of such funds. And do not be reticent about going to your congregation for financial assistance. It is in your congregation's self-interest that you have such a personal colleague group. In some ways, it is like having a multiple staff in your parish because you have a group of professionals who will assist you in problem solving and see you through some tough pastoral situations that cannot be shared with other members of the parish because they are so private.

In summary, these are my suggestions for putting together a quality support group for yourself:

1. Find one other person with whom you can launch a process for beginning a support group. Lay some basic plans with this person.

2. Decide between the two of you what would be the primary focus of the group. You may decide on one basic purpose, such as individual personal support for each of the members, and then have some secondary goals for the group, such as job placement or sermon preparation. I recommend that personal support always have priority over professional skill development. What most of us need is some help in dealing with the daily issues and problems that buffet us. Once we have dealt with these, we can handle some long-term problems.

3. Consider with this other person whom you would like to invite into this potentially intimate fellowship. The chemistry needs to be right or it won't work.

4. Think through a skeleton covenant to propose for the group. The covenant needs to address

    a. How often the group is to meet.
    b. How long group meetings are to be.
    c. Whether attendance at meetings is optional.
    d. Confidentiality.
    e. The length of the first covenant period.
    f. How meetings are to be critiqued.
    g. The basic format of each meeting.

The simplest way to get a basic covenant agreement is for one member to write out a first draft and then have others react to it. Keep in mind that some people may get nervous when too much gets nailed down before things really get started. Sometimes people need to sense whether the group feels right to them before they are willing to sign on for six months.

5. Mutually decide upon a group facilitator who can help your support group meet its objectives. Recall the three key characteristics of an effective group facilitator, namely that the person be competent, sensitive, and safe. Explore with that person whether he or she is willing to help you get this support group off the ground and how much compensation he or she would like to receive. Put together a budget based on this fee.

6. Set a time, place, and initial format for the first meeting. Then between the two of you send out the invitations and let the magic happen.

A word about place and initial format. It is always tempting for us as clergy to say, "Well, let's meet in my church." There is usually lots of comfortable space available in churches when clergy groups have time to meet. Meeting in a group member's church saves that person travel time. The drawback is the host pastor's difficulty in moving to extradependence. Even though host pastors may inform secretaries that they will not be available for the two-hour meeting period, it is simply too tempting to work right up until the time the group gathers. It is also too easy to walk down the hall at a break to see whether someone important returned a phone call. In short, the host pastor does not leave the work environment and thus can only partially get away from it all. It would be better to meet in neutral space so that everyone in the group can be fully present to the group.

It is also important to give some thought to the initial meeting. Groups move quickly into patterns of behavior. It's very difficult for us to function without norms, and the early behavior of group members can easily develop into group norms. The following are some areas of group life in which norms tend to be formed:

Dress
Language
Touching
Initial greetings
How differences are dealt with
Affection
Piety
Whether men and women are treated the same or differently
How gratitude is expressed
Confidentiality
Honesty and candor
Closure styles

It is possible to raise these areas of group life to the conscious level and have members talk about their preferences. Groups can consciously form norms to which they adhere in later life.

The two groups in which I am a regular participant have developed a norm that everyone hugs everyone else, both in greeting and in departing. It's a simple enough practice. Yet I believe it sets the tone for our meetings. It signals that we are there for one another. Try to start your group with warmth and affection, and I am confident your way of doing so will continue through the life of your group.

A Basic Format for a Two-Hour Meeting

Ingathering

These days it is unusual for people to gather without having some hot or cold drinks available. People should be able to pour themselves something to drink and then gather. Once people have greeted one another and are seated in a circle, they are often helped by a brief activity that allows them to lay down whatever they have brought with them into the

meeting and become fully present to the group. Some groups begin with
two or three minutes of silence during which people are able to center in
and become aware of what is going on inside of them. Introverts will
generally feel more like participating if they are given a few minutes of
silence before they are asked to speak.

The male awareness group I meet with usually begins with a five-
minute chant, followed by another five minutes of silence.[1] Reading a
portion of Scripture followed by a time of prayer or silence is yet another
way to start.

Sharing of Self

Group members may then take some air time to tell what has been occur-
ring in their personal or professional lives. Generally this happens best
when the facilitator offers a model, for example:

—"Let's take some time to talk about the highs and lows of our
lives since the last time we met."
— "On the road of life there are both potholes that jar us and scenes
of beauty. Let's each take some time to talk about the potholes
we've hit in the last few weeks, and also what scenes of beauty
we have encountered."
—"This time around, let's focus on the state of our souls. What's
been happening lately that has fed and nurtured our souls, and
what seems to continue to throw us off center?"
—"I'd like to suggest that today we listen to our bodies intensely
and try to determine what they are saying to us right now about
how we are managing life and ministry."
—"In this season of Lent we see Jesus setting forth toward
Jerusalem and facing the cross. What is the cross we are facing
or should be facing, and what is our hope for a resurrection that
is to follow?"
— "I'd like to suggest that this week we each take five minutes and
work with a sheet of newsprint to track the emotional and spiritual highs and lows of our past year. Put your emotional highs
and lows in a different color or use a different kind of line than
the one you use for your spiritual highs and lows. After that be
prepared to share this time line with the group."

This time of sharing will consume a major chunk of the two hours. The facilitator can have members take ten minutes each to talk using a model like those suggested, returning to those individuals who seem to be hurting the most and giving them some extra time. Or the facilitator can give some people more time than others, depending upon the perceived need of the individual. I prefer the first strategy because it gets everyone's life out on the table before allowing the energy to move to where there is the greatest pain or need.

Critique and Closure

Before everyone flies off to the four winds, it is important that some time and energy be given to finding out how the members feel about the quality of their life together and whether they are getting what they need from the group. Once again, the group facilitator provides a model for the group to reflect on its process. Some examples are the following:

—"How are we feeling about ourselves as a support group? What do you like about what's taking place here, and what concerns you about how we are relating?"
—"We are developing a rhythm in our life together. What do you like about the rhythm and what concerns you?"
—"I need to know if you are getting what you need from me as a group facilitator. What would you like more of from me? What would you like less of from me? What would you like me to keep on doing the same?"
—"Surprises are often a great way to monitor what is going on in a group. When something materializes that we didn't expect, that's a surprise, or when we expected things to happen in a certain way and they didn't, that's another type of surprise. What are the ways in which we are surprised by how this support group is developing?"
—"Let's take a little longer time to review the bidding related to this group. Could each one of us make a personal statement about how our expectations for this support group are being met, and are not being met?"

I strongly recommend that no group meeting end without at least a few minutes of closing reflection. When the group is rushed to get to appointments, a couple of minutes for people to reflect on how the group worked that day can be enough. Ideally, reflection will become so routine that it becomes ritualized. It is the one ingredient, that when built into a group, gives it the consistent capacity to shift gears in order to meet more fully the needs of its members. When there is no reflection built into the group life, people start missing meetings and everyone is confused about why the group is not meeting certain people's needs. Guessing at this is no substitute for encouraging candor from the beginning.

Finally, a closing ritual, even a brief one, has a way of helping members feel they are part of a group that is there for them. Another round of hugs is one such ritual. Ending with a chant or hymn sends people away with a song in their heart. A moment of silence helps people make the transition back into other realities. One image I have is that of a basketball team just before the first string takes the court. All the players grasp hands in the center and break with a shout. In a clergy support group, an Alleluia could replace the shout.

Starting Groups at a Middle Judicatory Level

The results of the research project in Carlisle Presbytery turned out to be so positive that I would advocate trying to replicate some of its key elements. The effort might begin with some basic research about how many clergy groups there are in your middle judicatory. You would need to assess the type and quality of these support communities.

A distinction must be made between a regularly called district meeting of clergy (Lutheran), the meeting of clergy within a deanery (Episcopal), or a group of area clergy (UCC), and what I call personal or professional support groups. The former are usually too large to support individual clergy in their pain and confusion. Also, some business matters are relegated to these larger groups, e.g., the election of a dean. I cannot deprecate the value of the former type of group. It often plays a very useful function in ministering to the needs of clergy in an area within the middle judicatory.

Beyond these larger administrative groups, how many ongoing clergy support groups are there in your middle judicatory? The answer to this question can help determine the target area for raising the morale and the professional effectiveness of clergy within your system. It is impossible to have all clergy in such support groups. The loners will always rebel. I think having half the clergy in support groups would be a worthwhile objective.

Start Groups with a Two-Day Retreat

If your middle judicatory has a tradition of holding an annual clergy conference, I would recommend preempting that event with a kickoff to the formation of more support groups in your system.

A two-day conference has the potential for assembling a critical mass of clergy in the middle judicatory. It can lay out the key advantages of effective peer support groups and point out the hazards of flying solo while doing parish ministry. The retreat can also do a thorough job of presenting the Oscillation Theory of the Grubb Institute and what constitutes helpful extradependence. This "dependency model" of support groups can be explored fully with participants. Finally, those at the retreat can begin making contact with persons they would like to have in such a collegial relationship. Once again, let's be clear that this kind of support group cannot be legislated, nor can it be formed for clergy. People need to enter group covenants voluntarily.

In planning this clergy conference, I would include five components that need to be present if clergy are to be offered a significant nudge in the direction of forming their own support systems.

1. The initial clergy conference must be attractive enough so that there is an above-average chance of getting a majority of the clergy in the system to attend. Sometimes this means getting a well-known keynote speaker who will become part of the draw.

2. The content of the retreat should focus on clergy health and wholeness, possibly with an emphasis on the destructive effects of stress and burnout on clergy followed by some ways clergy can take better care of themselves. Having a quality support group is then seen in context as a strong self-care strategy.

3. The Oscillation Theory, which emphasizes why parish ministry is such a demanding profession, can be presented. Clergy are constantly

taking care of others by providing them with extradependence, yet have few places where they themselves can move into extradependence. The Dependency model of support groups can then be explained with backup data from the Carlisle study.

4. Toward the end of the retreat, participants need to be encouraged to enter a process whereby they are given a chance to mill about talking with people or groups in an attempt to find the right combination of people for their support needs. This part of the retreat needs a minimum of one hour. People should be encouraged to explore genuinely more than one possible support community. Participants can also be encouraged to think about potential support group members who were not able to attend the retreat.

I am aware that this part of the retreat sounds as if it could fall on its face. When I got to this part of the retreat with the Carlisle Presbytery clergy, I was quite apprehensive that some people might get locked into groups too early, making for poor combinations; that all the darlings of the judicatory would cluster together, leaving others with unattractive groups; that some people would find themselves rejected from groups of their choosing; that others would simply be left out; or that no groups would form. Yet I knew of no other way of doing it; I needed to trust the process. To my amazement, clustering was exactly what was needed, and people seemed well satisfied with the combinations in the group of their choice. At the retreat in Carlisle Presbytery, persons made commitments to call those who were not present to invite them into their specific group. The proof of the pudding is in the eating: four new clergy groups formed as a result of that retreat, and all four were going strong at the end of three years of life together.

5. There should be a list of potential support group facilitators from which these groups can choose. It would be helpful if some prior contact could be made with these potential facilitators, getting some idea of their willingness to serve the church in this role and the kind of honorarium they think they would need for this leadership role.

Here the middle judicatory can also offer something of substance to assist these groups in getting underway, namely funds to subsidize the expense. I do not recommend total subsidy because I believe the participating clergy and their congregations need to own part of the expense. Their commitment to it will be stronger if this is the case. Yet some clergy living on limited funds may find their portion of the facilitator's fee prohibitive. Scholarship funds for them might be in order.

Of course, middle judicatories are also strapped for funds these days. They may not be able to afford this ministry to clergy out of budgeted funds. I would encourage you to seek some special funding for this separate cause. When confronted with a concrete way to support the ministry of the clergy in your system, individual donors would probably want to contribute; it is one specific way to assist those on the firing line of day-to-day parish ministry.

The Role of Facilitator

The model for an effective peer support group with clergy as advocated in this book is heavily dependent on an outside facilitator. I have come to call it a dependency model of support ministries. It is especially useful when working with occupations whose primary focus is the direct care of others. I could see this model working well with other professionals such as teachers, social workers, therapists, and police. Parents with children of the same age could also find great healing through this format for a support group.

Clergy too easily miss this point about needing an outside facilitator and claim they do not need one. After all, they argue, don't they work with groups all the time and have skills enough to spare? I believe that is the point. Clergy of all types should know that managing a group takes work. Anyone trying to chair a meeting in which a group needs to work through some controversial issues to arrive at a decision knows what I am talking about here.

The model, which builds heavily upon the Oscillation Theory of the Grubb Institute, claims that no one moves to a state of extradependence until they perceive that there is strength at the center of the experience. When a group of clergy meet on a Monday afternoon, where is the strength at the center of their group, allowing people to let go and just be for a while? And without strong leadership at the center of the group I do not believe any of the members will risk revealing what is really happening in their lives. Group trust depends on strong, reliable leadership at the center. If that does not come from an outside facilitator who possesses the three qualities of competence, sensitivity, and safety, from where is it going to come?

The inevitable response from most clergy is: Can't one of us be the leader of the group? The answer is always, Yes. Yet the follow-up question needs to be: What will it cost that person to take over the leadership role? This pastor goes from taking care of parishioners all week to taking care of peers when that support group meets. For this group is not likely to be a healing experience for that pastor because he or she is working throughout the group time.

What about members sharing leadership? It's a fair question, but the chances are high that it won't work. What groups need to move to trust is stability of leadership. If the leadership role rotates from one member to another and each one's leadership style is different, the group will have difficulty trusting the process.

A concrete example of how this model fails to work with shared leadership comes out of my experience working with the United States Army Chaplain Corps. An army base may have four to six chaplains. Each one is a chaplain to each special unit at the base. Yet on Sunday morning there may be only one chapel service, which army personnel can attend with their families. Normally one chaplain is placed in charge of each chapel, with the other chaplains being there to assist on Sunday morning. At one of the bases where I was conducting research, I discovered an experiment that was being carried out at one of the Protestant chapels. There were five chaplains on the post, and they decided not to put one of the chaplains in charge of the chapel but to allow each of the chaplains to rotate the responsibility on Sundays. This meant that every Sunday morning the congregation would have a different chaplain leading in worship. When chaplains were not leading in worship that Sunday, they had the day off. Few of them chose to worship with the congregation when they were not leading in worship. The result of the experiment was that over a six-month period the attendance at that chapel service dropped from an average Sunday congregation of 350 to forty-five. With the chaplains rotating pastoral leadership, the congregation felt abandoned; there was no one pastor who cared for them on a Sunday-to-Sunday basis. As a result, they went somewhere else to get their extra-dependency needs met.

When everyone takes turns at leadership the group is, in essence, leaderless. It just won't work. Where it does work, the group is pretending to share leadership, but at some level of consciousness all the members know that if things get too chaotic, Bill will step in and lead the group through the difficulty. What's more, the group will not realize how much they really do depend on Bill to take care of them when the going gets tough, or how that role diminishes Bill's ability to get his support needs met from the group. Better to admit that there is a job to be done here and that this job is no minor role if the group is to function well. It's more honest to contract for an outsider to perform that role and to reimburse him or her for the work.

My own discovery of the important role of facilitators was rather traumatic. While working for the Lutherans in Pennsylvania I had the title "assistant to the bishop." In many ways for clergy in that synod, I was not a safe person to whom to reveal sensitive information. My loyalty was to my bishop and to the work of the synod. Clergy in that system sensed something about me that I did not know about myself. If my bishop had asked me about recommending any of them for another pastorate, I would have told him everything I knew about that person. Thus, I could affect the career opportunities of any of the clergy with whom I worked. It was not in their self-interest to have me know something negative about them. I can remember the frustration of always feeling this barrier between me and the clergy with whom I worked. I responded with negative feelings about clergy in general. They were so careful with me that I concluded many of them were gutless wonders without a whole lot of commitment to the mission of the church, especially on social justice issues.

I left that job to go work for the Metropolitan Ecumenical Training Center in Washington, D.C. I was to complete a foundation-funded project that focused on developing models to help clergy become clearer about their continuing education needs. To do that job, I asked to meet with a group of no more that ten clergy from each of four denominations in the area. I met with them once a month for a year to assist them in becoming more intentional and specific about their professional development. What took place in each of those groups over the course of a year absolutely astounded me. It was like a conversion experience. Without having realized it, I had become the safe, outside person on whom they could become extradependent. The candor level of each of those groups was what struck me most. Those clergy started to lay out their lives in ways I had not heard before. My whole view of clergy began to turn around through the course of that year. Suddenly, I was put back in touch with the pain and confusion arising from the pastor's complex role. The other thing that impressed me deeply was the bonding that took place. After twelve years, I still find myself thinking about two of those four groups, remembering well the closeness that developed in them. It was a sad day when the money from the grant ran out and I had to turn to other projects. As it was, I went on facilitating one of those groups for six months simply because I knew the group would fold when I withdrew my leadership, and I didn't have the heart to draw the curtain.

Thus, from firsthand experience, as well as from the Carlisle Project, I know it works. Somewhere in the back of my mind I keep thinking that this is what I would like to do once I retire from being a senior consultant for The Alban Institute. If there were any way that I could promise a group of clergy that I could be present with them on a monthly basis, I might even consider it now. Several years ago I had a request from a group of Episcopal clergy in Washington, D.C., to be their support group facilitator. As attractive as the opportunity was, I could not, given my contract and travel schedule, promise them the kind of continuity they needed. The role of facilitator can be a practical, valuable way of being a pastor to pastors. Of course, the facilitator speaks relatively little. The role really involves helping group members "unpack their stuff" so the group can give them support and perspective and constantly paying attention to what is happening both to individuals and to the group as a whole. Being able to offer this help to a group of church professionals under siege is a real gift.

All the members of the group need to do is to show up on time. They don't need to give any thought to what is to take place at the meeting. They can come in panting, grab a cup of coffee, and plop themselves into a chair. It is the facilitator who then takes charge and says, "All right, we are all here. Let's take a moment to be quiet and become centered. As you engage in some deep breathing, I invite you for a moment to see yourself as God sees you, through the eyes of Grace." After a few minutes, the facilitator takes charge again and asks each person to talk about the baggage they bring to the group that day and when there have been moments of Grace for them in the past week. Wow! What a gift. All people had to do was to arrive, and in minutes they are revealing the deep places in their lives.

This is not to say that the facilitator does all the work of loving everyone in the group. Members need to reach out to touch and support their brothers or sisters when they are in pain. Yet there is a clear difference between letting my love pour out naturally when I feel it and trying to figure out what I need to do to help this person. It is the facilitator's job to pay attention to who is getting too much attention and who is not getting enough, and what appears to be helping someone and what is not. In short, the facilitator helps members direct and channel their caring for one another in ways that will be most productive. It's the facilitator who goes home at night thinking about whether what the group did for someone today was the best it could have for them and how the group might be of greater assistance next time. The other group members, after a brief closing ritual, jump back into their work and don't need to think about the group again (unless they find themselves naturally checking in on somebody the following week) until the next meeting. And if during the group meeting their mind wanders off for a minute, they are confident that someone else is minding the store while they are gone.

Good facilitators are worth their weight in gold. A facilitator will be working hard the entire time your group meets and should be reimbursed in some way for the effort. That person will often make the difference between a group with depth and richness and one that is as deep as a rain puddle, more a drain on participants' energy than a boost. I cannot urge you strongly enough—*do not cheat yourself by thinking you can spare the expense and do without a facilitator.*

NOTES

1. Some beautiful chants on audiocassette may be obtained from Life Structure Resources, Box 212, Boonsboro, MD 21713. Phone (301) 432-6054.

CHAPTER VI

Implications for Lay Groups within Your Congregation

The Need

There will always be people within a congregation who at certain times in their lives need more personal support than they can receive from their congregation as a whole. This is especially true in larger congregations, those with an average Sunday attendance of 150 or more. Depending on the specific needs of these people, they are often very grateful to be part of smaller support groups that speak to their needs. In addition, their loyalty and commitment to the congregation increases proportionally to the quality of the support offered. When the congregation is there for them in their need, they, in turn, will be there for the congregation in its need.

For some the need is related to personal health. For example, persons with cancer will probably be eager join of a group of people who have had cancer and survived or who are learning to cope with the disease. People with weight problems are often helped by such groups as Weight Watchers. Some people are able to remain part of an exercise program largely because they exercise with other people; in these cases, it is as much the company as it is the routine that keeps people coming back.

In confronting an addiction, a support group is almost mandatory. The power of any twelve-step program is mainly in the group meetings and the individual support that grows out of the relationships formed at those meetings.

The hospice movement is based on the concept of giving support to those who are dying and their families. Hospitals are some of the worst places to die. A death is considered a failure in a hospital; hence little support is there for helping people face death with dignity and purpose.

Support groups for those who are unemployed can make the difference between perseverance or giving up. A colleague of mine who survived eighteen months of unemployment with surprisingly good humor credits his sanity to a group of people that met weekly in a church. He claims he is unafraid to face unemployment again because of what he learned about himself and the process of finding a job from this support group.

Support groups with titles such as "Single Again" are geared to those experiencing the loss of a marital relationship. Many find that it is not the end of the world to have loved and lost. Gender-specific groups addressing this issue can often be even more helpful because men and women appear to need a different quality of support following this loss of a relationship.

Men's awareness groups have risen in popularity most recently. Men are beginning to benefit from the same types of groups that have supported the consciousness-raising of women for the past decade. Men have become aware that the macho image is bankrupt, yet they remain unclear about other models of maleness. Men have also begun to value their feelings and experiences and want to be connected with other men who share their growth journey.

Women often have such effective informal networking skills that they fail to commit themselves to a specific group that meets regularly to support them in their journey. Women are often helped by the perspective a group can give them as they try to move forward in careers that depend on succeeding in a hierarchical system dominated by white males.

A colleague of mine here at The Alban Institute, Celia Hahn, together with her husband Bob, is part of a parish support group called the White Water Group. Five couples felt that marriage was more like navigating white water in a raft than paddling around a quiet pool. The couples found their support group particularly helpful in dealing with teen-aged children. Being with other parents helped them feel that they were not going crazy and that others experienced difficulties with adolescents. Celia reports that at one time there were twelve support groups for couples in her church.

Spiritual hunger can also be mitigated by groups that are willing to explore specific spiritual practices. People often overlook how fear can seriously hinder people from moving deeper into spiritual awareness. The practice of meditation, for example, can often be greatly supported by the presence of a group. Some can't understand why anyone would travel for thirty minutes or more just to sit in silence with other people. Yet fear of going deeper into the unknown often blocks people from trying to meditate on their own. The same can be true of other prayer forms and spiritual disciplines.

Groups can also provide the support people seek when they take their ministry in the world seriously. We clergy talk a great game about lay ministries yet consistently find them difficult to support in regular, substantial ways. Not everyone feels called to lay ministries. In fact, few seem willing to admit that they are. Yet what a gift it is to offer support to those who feel they need more from their church to face the difficulties and complexities of being agents of peace and healing to a broken world through their daily vocation. The realization that other people in the parish know what your call is seems to be gift enough. To have those same people rooting for you, being there for you when you feel you fail, and praying for you as you try again is to add grace upon grace.

In short, the needs are endless. It is only a question of there being enough people in the parish facing the same difficulty at the same time or needing a similar type of support. Monitoring those needs and gathering people together accordingly can be ongoing yet important work. It's an effective way of being pastoral to members, namely helping them connect with others who have similar needs.

But connecting is only half the battle. Simply herding people with similar needs together and hoping that they will make something out of that grouping is to set them up for disappointment and failure. Facilitating the process of their coming together with focus and trust is yet another big step toward providing them with a quality support experience within the parish.

The Process

Leaderless groups don't work. Although we might like to herd a group of people together and have them become a support network, this strategy does not work any better than that of a church executive trying to herd a group of clergy together with the hope that they will develop into an in-depth support community.

To achieve depth and quality in any small group experience within your congregation, the Oscillation Theory and the concept of extradependence must be taken seriously. If a Bible study or a prayer or meditation group is to function without your presence, lay leaders must be trained and supported for this ministry. This means that, in addition to having expertise in biblical study or prayer or meditation, these leaders must be willing and able to take charge and become group facilitators. They need to learn how to become a "good enough religious authority" in whose presence others can move to a state of extradependence. Here again, these lay leaders need to be competent, sensitive, and safe. Without these characteristics trust is unlikely to develop and, as a result, members of those groups are not likely to reveal their pain and vulnerability. Members will then look to you as pastor as the one on whom they can depend for this kind of extradependence. In a parish where more than 150 people regularly attend Sunday worship, this can quickly lead to burnout.

To develop lay leaders with the skill and desire to facilitate quality small groups in your parish, the same kinds of questions that clergy support groups face must be addressed. Where will these lay leaders get their extradependence needs met so that they come to their group ministries with cups that are full rather than empty most of the time? In short, are there ways to provide spiritual nurture for these lay leaders so that they do not seek to have their extradependence needs met in the groups they are leading? Is it possible for them to be part of other groups in which someone is paying attention to their primary needs so that they are then able to turn around and do the same for others?

Here the training of these leaders and their continued nurture can take place in parallel. You as pastor can act as facilitator of a group of potential lay facilitators, leading them in a process that they will eventually facilitate for others.

The first step in developing lay facilitators is discovering those in the parish who feel called to the ministry of group facilitating. It is a fulfilling ministry that can highlight skills learned elsewhere. Yet group process skills are best used by people who understand the power that a quality support group can have and who have the capacity to care for these groups. It is a ministry that can transform people's lives, and it requires people who have caught the vision and are willing to make personal sacrifices for these transformation groups to come alive.

A possible way to begin lay groups is to personally invite into a group those members of the congregation who you believe have the gift for this kind of ministry or might feel so called. The number invited should be small enough so that you could genuinely offer them an experience of personal support through extradependence. You as pastor would be the group facilitator. Over the course of six to twelve months, you would not only be facilitating the support group for them, but you would be training them in the process. The Oscillation Theory of the Grubb Institute should be a key theory studied in the group. People could reflect on when they felt themselves in a state of extradependence and when not. A regular critique of the process and your role as facilitator would be keys to learning.

From that group you could then choose those whom you believed were skilled and called to the ministry of group facilitating. These persons could then call into community a specific group of people who share a special need.

For example, you as pastor could say, "John, there is a handful of people I know of in this congregation who feel called to their daily vocation. They seem to be wanting something more from the parish than I or the congregation as a whole is able to give. I would like you to take the initiative and call these people together. Let's set it up as a three-month experiment. I will be at the first meeting to explain the experiment and the process. Does this sound like a ministry you could become committed to, namely providing a structure through which these people could support each other in their lay ministry?"

Or

"Mary, we have a group of single mothers in this parish who really seem to be struggling with their lot in life. Mainly they are exhausted with trying to manage both home and work, yet they also feel isolated and unsupported. There probably are ways in which they could be of real help to one another. How would you feel about calling them together and exploring with them the formation of a support group? Let's structure the group to meet on Sunday morning during the Sunday school hour. I'll help you call the group together and get it going."

Or

"Jane, I know of three women in this parish who have recently discovered that they have breast cancer. They are going to need some special attention in the next six months. How would you feel about calling this group together and facilitating their meeting regularly over the next few months? Mary Jones would probably love to have the group meet in her home."

Or

"Bill, General Electric is shutting down its plant here in the city, and I know of eight of our members who will be facing a layoff. A few feel they have some options, but most are facing the unknown. How would you feel about calling that group together, plus any others we have in the parish who want to consider a vocational change? Let's see if we can get a ministry going here in the parish focused on those facing a job search. It could be a way of reaching out to nonmembers of this congregation as well."

Having a cadre of trained facilitators is like having money in the bank that can be invested in key opportunities. Care would need to be taken to see that these facilitators continue to feel called to these ministries and that they are getting their support needs met elsewhere in the parish. As pastor you would be wise to remain vigilant in the spiritual nurture of these facilitators. You might consider continuing as group facilitator to the support group made up of these facilitators.

Once a facilitator had a group functioning and it seemed that the group was developing rituals that could keep it alive and healthy, those norms and rituals could fulfill a leadership function. Then the facilitator could be withdrawn and plugged into another emerging group. The critical issue would be whether the group's members continued to commit themselves to addressing the need or pain of persons in the parish or the neighborhood.

In Conclusion

In Romans 12:5, Paul talks about us being "members one of another" within the body of Christ. He is talking about a reality that many people rarely experience simply because they have never really been a part of a deeply caring community. In this book I have tried to lay out a process that I know works for making this spiritual reality one that more people can experience firsthand.

My main concern has been for clergy support groups. I am anxious when I see so many clergy flying solo, unaware of their need for support or unable to garner that support when they know they need it. I am particularly pained when I see clergy burning out because they continually give to others while receiving so little. When the symptoms of burnout become obvious and they cast their eyes about to see who is supporting them in their efforts, they find nothing of substance coming their way. The disillusionment they feel often spells the end of their ministry.

Conversely, I hold a vision of clergy in solid peer support groups providing a strong network that undergirds their lives and ministry, who then in turn begin building support communities within their congregations so that people really feel cared for in their need. This is my image of what the church is about on this side of Glory. I am in the church today because I have experienced this support when I least expected it. It came from within the believing fellowship. I also carry the scars of being wounded by total lack of support at some crucial times in my ministry. I believe I know about the support process because I've experienced both in its absence and its fulfillment.

What I've learned is that quality support communities do not happen by accident. They require hard work. Leadership is key to our intentionality about building support communities. Without leadership there is no strength at the center of these groups. Without strength at the center, few of us will risk revealing our personal pain and confusion. Why have a support group if you cannot be open about your pain and confusion?

The theory that shed the most light on this process for me is Bruce Reed's Oscillation Theory and the distinction he makes between states of intradependence and extradependence. This explains more about why some groups work and others don't than any other theory available. I'm grateful to Carlisle Presbytery for the chance to test this theory with clergy groups in their area. I welcome the opportunity to test this theory ecumenically in several metropolitan areas on this continent.

BIBLIOGRAPHY

Cherniss, Cary. *Staff Burnout.* Beverly Hills: Sage Publications, 1980.

Bellah, Robert N. *Habits of the Heart.* New York: Harper & Row, 1986.

Spencer, Sabina A. and Adams, John D. *Life Changes.* San Luis Obispo, CA 93406: Impact Publishers, 1990.

Reed, Bruce. *Dynamics of Religion.* London: Darton, Longman and Todd, 1978.

___. *Task of the Church and the Role of its Members.* Washington, DC: The Alban Institute, Inc., 1975.

Sagan, Leonard A. *The Health of Nations.* Basic Books, 1987.

Sanford, John A. *Ministry Burnout.* Mahwah, NJ: Paulist Press, 1982.

Jacobson, MD, Edmund. *You Must Relax.* New York: McGraw Hill Paperbacks, 1978, 5th edition.

The Alban Institute:
an invitation to membership

The Alban Institute, begun in 1979, believes that the congregation is essential to the task of equipping the people of God to minister in the church and the world. A multi-denominational membership organization, the Institute provides on-site training, educational programs, consulting, research, and publishing for hundreds of churches across the country.

The Alban Institute invites you to be a member of this partnership of laity, clergy, and executives—a partnership that brings together people who are raising important questions about congregational life and people who are trying new solutions, making new discoveries, finding a new way of getting clear about the task of ministry. The Institute exists to provide you with the kinds of information and resources you need to support your ministries.

Join us now and enjoy these benefits:

Action Information, a highly respected journal published 6 times a year, to keep you up to date on current issues and trends.

Inside Information, Alban's quarterly newsletter, keeps you informed about research and other happenings around Alban. Available to members only.

Publication Discounts:

- ☐ 15% for Individual, Retired Clergy, and Seminarian Members
- ☐ 25% for congregational members
- ☐ 40% for Judicatory and Seminary Executive Members

Discounts on Training and Education Events

Write our Membership Department at the address below, or call us at (202) 244-7320 for more information about how to join The Alban Institute's growing membership, particularly about Congregational Membership in which 12 designated persons receive all benefits of membership.

The Alban Institute, Inc.
4125 Nebraska Avenue NW
Washington, DC 20016